Russia in 1990s
Sunset of the Soviet Socialism

Irina Lobatcheva

Parallel Worlds' Books

Copyright © 2013 Irina Lobatcheva

All rights reserved

ISBN: 1493655256

ISBN-13: 9781493655250

CONTENTS

Preface	1
The Beginning	7
Perestroika	13
August 1991 Coup	23
Privatization	29
Criminalization of Russia	33
The Russian Parliament is Defeated	36
Parliament Fell Victim of Yeltsin's Lust for Power	69
Reporters Abandoned Even the Pretense of Objectivity	77
No Man In a Prophet in His Own Country	79
Epilogue	82
Russian in Numbers	83
Works Cited	84

PREFACE

I am Russian. My family suffered from Stalin's repressions: my grandfather, arrested by NKVD on a fake accusation in 1937, had never returned to his wife and eight children, leaving them, ostracized as traitors, to fend for themselves. Nonetheless, I have to admit that I miss the gone-forever Soviet Union.

In 1960s-1980s the Soviet society provided majority of Russians with a decent life, free of fear of unemployment, with plenty of opportunities for self-fulfillment and career advancement. Everyone had a right to a month long vacation which one could spend in recreation hotels, sanatoriums, or touring the USSR for a very affordable price. Medical care was free, as well as any education, numerous children clubs and summer camps; even day-care centers cost next to nothing. Simple life, overall confidence in the future, guaranteed pension. The ideological load had almost waned after the death of Stalin: the state security had little effect on our lives compared to its influence in 1930s-1950s, when harsh competition with the rest of the world demanded from the new socialist state extraordinary repressive measures. Socialistic economy was more humane than any other in the history of mankind, and because of that more prone to failure.

Apparently, the Soviet socialism was a rare fluke that needed to be cherished and treasured as a political experiment on one-fifth of the world territory. Russia had tested one of the ways - the Soviet way - of reaching Utopia, a communist world that realizes the principle *from each according to his ability, to each according to his needs*. We did not save socialism and committed the greatest of the sins: we scared off many of its potential followers, as noted by prominent Russian philosopher Aleksandr Zinoviev in his book *The Russian Tragedy (The Death of Utopia)*.

It is generally believed that the decline of the Soviet socialism began about thirty years ago when the Soviet Union started losing the arms race to the United States and headed into the crisis of development. The Soviet politicians and economists refused to admit and deal with it, because they believed to Karl Marx, who declared that socialism progressed crisis-free. The Soviet socialism was a unique social phenomenon, and nobody knew how to fix its ills. This partially explains the failed reforms of Mikhail Gorbachev, then current Soviet leader. The unresolved crisis had caused a collapse of the Soviet planned economy and socialism; its successor - a laissez-faire free market - drove Russia into the great depression of 1990s.

Participants and eye-witnesses of turbulent events in Russia of 1990s are passing away. Authorities change history the way they need, shifting accents, keeping silence on some circumstances and bumping others to prominence. This is the story of how Russia happened to swerve from the path of social justice, as seen through the eyes of an ordinary Russian.

THE BEGINNING

Mid of 1980s. The communist party played an enormous role in our life. At every Soviet enterprise, every social organization, in any town or village there were official representatives of the communist party, which controlled the execution of plans set by the Soviet government. Not everyone could become a party-man. Members of the party were the most socially active citizens of the Soviet society. Though some of them were just social climbers, majority did not make party membership their career and had no benefits from their affiliation. They performed community service without monetary compensation. Members of the party interfered in all facets of business of their companies and held behavior of workers and their superiors within certain moral norms. The primary party cells adhered to democratic principles, sending delegates to the conferences, where the administrative apparatus was formed. The trade unions, which were also plentiful, dealt with recreational activities of employees. By Yeltsin's November 1991's decree, any activity of the Communist Party of the USSR was banned and all its administrative units were dissolved, thus the biggest social organization of the Russian population in was forever liquidated.

Reforms and restructuring started in 1986. The adoption of "more advanced" free market and democratic principles of governing had resulted in a drastic impoverishment of the majority of people, so that in 1990's the Russian population was shrinking by almost a million citizens annually. And we, ordinary Russians, enthusiastically participated in peaceful demolition of the world superpower into a poverty-stricken country.

At the end of 1970's - beginning of 1980's nothing hinted at the upcoming collapse of the Soviet Union. The Soviet economy planned, manufactured, distributed, and provided us with everything necessary to have a decent and unpretentious life. It is difficult to imagine how it was possible, in the absence of powerful computers, to control the production and distribution of goods down to the level of kilograms of nails and number of paper clips in the largest country of the world. Obviously, the planning system did not cope with its responsibilities seamlessly, but it worked. The country managed to evolve; no one was hungry or jobless. After the war with Germany, the Soviet population had grown by one hundred million people. And the state was making colossal efforts to provide its people with decent living conditions.

If socialism in the Soviet Union had lasted until the time of wide computerization, the management and planning processes would have been greatly improved, and the crisis of development might have been overcome. Though western economists believe that central planning is impossible in principle, the Soviet Union proved that it worked for over fifty years at least in one country, territorially the biggest in the world. Central planning is probably as hard as weather predictions, but nobody claims that the weather predictions are theoretically impossible.

Unfortunately, the decade of 1980s turned to be extremely infelicitous for the Soviet Union, aggravating the crisis and multiplying the problems. Oil, gas and mineral fertilizers - the source of foreign currency - had been sharply devaluated by the world market. The state let itself be involved in the civil war in Afghanistan supporting Babrak Karmal's government, continued an expensive arms race with the Western powers, and then had to cope with the Chernobyl disaster (1986) and devastating Spitak earthquake (1988), which killed 45,000 people and left 500,000 homeless. The country's economy did not produce enough consumer goods, because the "light" industry received insufficient funding. The government had no foreign currency to buy commodities abroad in order to reduce the shortage of supply at home; this caused a permanent and progressing lack of goods on the internal market, and people accumulated money in their thrift-boxes and on their accounts in the only Russian bank - SberBank. To cover cash deficit, the government had turned on its printing press, which would have led to higher prices on goods, had it been the free market economy. But the

Soviet government kept the internal prices at the level of 1961 y. (the year of the monetary reform that altered the price scale 10:1) for thirty years - the top officials feared that a rise in the level of prices of goods and services in peaceful time, when the country was not at war, would anger the population.

If the prices had been raised in the mid 80s, people would have understood and accepted the temporary hardship. We knew that the government was seeking funds to oppose all the mishaps and disasters. However, somebody at the top had underestimated our loyalty and had not ventured to adjust the prices early enough, letting the crisis inflate until the state imploded. For several years the state was just printing money without providing goods. Keeping the prices low, the government let the inflation transform into the total deficit of everything. And the hidden inflation grew like an avalanche, manifesting itself in lengthening queues even for food products of vital necessity...

In 1980s, meat, sausages, chocolate, coffee were gone from the store shelves seemingly forever. But the stores were not completely empty. The country still produced sturdy and unsightly clothing and shoes, cereals and bread, machine tools and weapons. The severity of the situation with the extreme shortage of food products in the end of 1980s had been somewhat corrected by the coupon system: to buy a scarce commodity it was necessary not only to pay the money, but also to show a special ticket to the cashier. The coupons or stamps for tobacco, vodka, sausage, butter, tea, sugar, soap, shampoo, detergents, etc. could be obtained from your municipality, if you were registered there as a resident. Coupons for durable goods were raffled off at the workplaces. One family member (of any age) was eligible to receive per month 0.5 kg of butter, 1 kg of sausages, and a bottle of vodka. At the time vodka and sausages were better currency than rubles. The shortage of everything in the late 1980's was terribly annoying, but not catastrophic. We did not starve, did not walk naked, and did not freeze in winter.

The most popular and well-off people were those who worked in sales and distribution of goods in short supply: employees of warehouses, depots, sales people in stores, as well as their relatives and friends. We did not "buy" things at the time; we procured, hunted for them via acquaintances.

Right networking meant a good life. You provide me with sausages and goodies - I'll pay you back with books in high demand or access to travelling abroad.

Somehow we all had adapted to a life of the total deficit, but still wondered: why at the time of peace, progress in science and technology and space travel we had to stand in five-hour long queues for soap and shampoo? Had it been like that all over the world, we would have endured the hardship. But in other countries of the socialist camp, not to mention developed Western states, the goods were in a much smaller shortage. There was something wrong with the Soviet Union. We still remembered relatively prosperous 1970s, and it was difficult to come to terms with the continuing decline of living standards in the 1980s.

Typical jokes of the time went something like this:

In Tbilisi a school teacher asks his first grade students about occupations of their fathers.
"My dad is a merchandiser," one says.
"My dad is a director of a warehouse," another boasts.
"My Dad is an engineer," says the third, and the class bursts out laughing.
"Children," the teacher reprimands, "it's not polite to laugh at someone else's misfortune!"

"Which hell is better - capitalistic or socialistic?"
"Of course, socialistic: either matches are gone, or fuel is in shortage, or boilers are under repair, or the devils have a party meeting."

There is a race between two sprinters: Soviet vs. American. The American had won. A Soviet newspaper reported: "In the sprint, the Soviet athlete finished among the first. The American runner was second to last."

PERESTROIKA

Death of the General Secretary of the Communist Party Leonid Brezhnev was first in a series of deaths of the Soviet Union's leaders in 1980s. Leonid Brezhnev ruled the Soviet empire from 1964 till 1982. His demise made us fear about our future: the good era of stability had come to an end. Brezhnev was succeeded by Yuri Andropov, then by Konstantin Chernenko (both of them soon died), and by Mikhail Gorbachev in 1985. Gorbachev was a politician of a younger generation and the main initiator of the "perestroika" and the politics of "new thinking"; he had ended Russian military presence in Afghanistan, reunified East and West Germany, started restructuring of the Soviet economy in order to saturate the internal market with consumer goods. Gorbachev's reforms returned to life private businesses in the form of cooperatives.

In Stalin's Russia there existed a strong private sector - the cooperatives, which produced all kinds of consumer goods from food products to high-tech and quickly reacted to the changing demands of the Soviet market. They employed about two million people and produced up to 6% of the total state GDP. But when Nikita Khrushchev came to power, he expropriated the cooperative's property for a nominal fee, and by 1960 majority of them had ceased to exist. Only private businesses, owned and run by one individual, were allowed to operate under the watchful eye of the militsiya. But the cooperatives did not vanish completely; some of them transformed into illegal private enterprises, where gangs of workers manufactured "under-the-table" surplus products from residues or stolen materials using state facilities and sold them secretly through the state-owned stores. In the Soviet Union such criminal gangs were called "tsehoviki". Mikhail Gorbachev's reforms legalized their businesses and launched new cooperatives. The unsaturated Soviet market consumed everything. The laws during "perestroika" were changing every month; no one knew what was allowed and what wasn't, and smart people successfully fished in troubled waters. Most of truly big Russian businesses started in 1980s, at the beginning of transformation of the Soviet socialism into capitalism.

Artyom Tarasov, a successful cooperator, who launched one of the first cooperatives in the Gorbachev's times, told his story at the famous TV show "Glance" in 1989. He confessed to earning 3,000,000 rubles per month as the head of a cooperative, which was in business of household appliance repairs (at the time average monthly salary was fewer than 300 rubles).[1] Tarasov instantly became famous. Later he wrote a book, in which he revealed origin of wealth of a typical Russian oligarch: energy and petroleum products' trade.[2] In Tarasov's case it happened like that: he learned that the Kremenchug Oil Refinery poured excess of mazut (low quality heavy fuel oil) into pits that the factory workers dug out in a nearby forest. The refinery's regular clients refused to buy mazut that winter, because the weather was warm. The refinery had no place to store the surplus, and they threw off about one million tons of mazut, wasting ninety million dollars on that. The refinery was not allowed selling its surplus oil abroad; in pre-Gorbachev's time, the foreign trade occurred exclusively through the State Foreign Trade Organization's channels, but Gorbachev abolished the state monopoly on the foreign trade and permitted private businesses to exchange primary resources abroad for consumer goods. In exchange for oil, metals and fertilizers, the cooperators imported personal computers, beer, cigarettes, chicken legs, and clothes. Thus, private businesses started uncontrollable export of raw materials, heaping prices in the world market; at the same time they imported those consumer products, which were cheapest in the developed countries and scarcest in the Soviet Union.

Tarasov signed a contract with the Kremenchug Oil Refinery, found a foreign buyer, and sent abroad the first tanker with over thirty thousand tons of mazut; this deal had brought Tarasov almost a million dollars, which he immediately used to import second-hand "Mercedes-Benz" cars.

Meanwhile, Gorbachev continued to unbalance the Soviet economy: he had abridged planning and distribution and essentially disconnected the suppliers and the manufacturers.

The Kremenchug Oil Refinery's warehouses were overstocked with petroleum products, and its top management bowed to the ground before Artyom Tarasov, when he emptied their warehouses, paying a few cents per ton of oil. The energy commodities Tarasov easily converted abroad into computers and cars without violating foreign trade articles of the Soviet Criminal Code. Each contract yielded about 1200% return on investment, and Tarasov's cooperative worked on up to seventy contracts at the same time. At the time, Soviet businessmen were not interested in saving dollars on bank accounts abroad, because foreign currency's use in the country was heavily restricted.

Corruption was the most difficult problem in Tarasov's work. Authorities were issuing oil export licenses in exchange for bribes; but even with the export license on hands, he had to pay other state officials involved in the process. For example, when a tanker goes to the port for load, a dispatcher could put it ahead of the queue or at the tail. So, Tarasov had to bribe the port manager, otherwise he would pay thousands of dollars in fines for a week of downtime. For pumping of oil to the port he also had to pay extra. The oil pipe usually passed through seven-eight regions of Russia; to deliver oil to the port without buying the "consent" of the local authorities was impossible. If transportation was via railroad, he or his representatives had to pay extra at each junction station, otherwise his cargo train would be driven into a dead end as if by chance. So whatever cargo he had on the road - a tank, a wagon, or the entire train, his men accompanied it with briefcases full of cash. And when his cargo finally reached the customs, there were rules, too: issuance of a customs declaration could take twenty minutes or ten days depending on the size of his gift, and the customs warehouses were prohibitively expensive. Tarasov did earn 1200% profit, but he had to share it with the placemen. These days of 1000% profits are gone. Now, according to economist Mikhail Khazin, businesses in Russia earn on average 30% profit.

Understandably, many people tried to get its share in the export of resources; it was much more profitable than developing a manufacturing business. At the time, the domestic prices on raw materials in the Soviet Union were several orders of magnitude lower than the world prices and were controlled by the state. And the less was the degree of processing of the raw materials, the higher was the profit from export, because of incompatibility of the Soviet and Western processing technologies. Of course, ordinary people had zero chances to enter the export of cheap petroleum and minerals. One needed to have acquaintances among directors of mines or refineries, railroad or port managers or captains of tankers; one needed to have connections with foreign buyers or the commodity market brokers, as well as initial capital to crank the very first deal.

Abolition of the state monopoly on foreign trade had created a "black hole" in the Soviet economy: the global market sucked in almost all cheap primary resources and completely destroyed the roughly balanced Soviet economy. No wonder that despite the Gorbachev's reforms and perestroika, domestic production of consumer goods continued to fall and the volume of imported goods was insufficient to meet the demand. Cooperatives had not solved the problem of the trade deficit. Any reasonable quality product landing store shelves was sold out in a matter of hours; every day thousands of people from central Russia arrived by trains to Moscow and stormed the capital's grocery stores. They grabbed whatever was on the shelves and, laden with shopping bags and heavy rucksacks, hurried back to the train stations. The country was sinking deeper and deeper into the abyss of the chronic consumer goods deficit and general economic crisis.

It would seem that anyone knowing how to make something would have no trouble selling his products in any quantities on the non-saturated Soviet market. But for a number of reasons it did not happen.

In March of 1990, the Supreme Soviet of People's Deputies of the USSR (the top power in the country) elected Mikhail Gorbachev the President of the Soviet Union, in addition to his post of the General Secretary of the Communist Party. Nearly a third of the deputies voted against him - this result had demonstrated "success" of his reforms. The country seethed; tens of thousands of strikes took place in 1990. Stratification of people by wealth, started with legalization of the cooperatives, came into conflict with the socialist idea of equality - a parity of earnings.

By the end of 1990, Soviet people accumulated 568 billion rubles on their accounts, and only 13% of that amount was secured by goods (in 1970 - 62%, for comparison), as was noted by Prime Minister of Russia Yegor Gaidar in his book *Collapse of an Empire: Lessons for Modern Russia*.[3] People could not invest cash in real estate, because the land belonged to the state, or in a new automobile - the queue of people willing to buy a car stretched for many years; it was impossible to convert money into foreign currency - possession of it was punishable by up to twelve years in prison. People saved money because they could not spend it.

In 1990, Gorbachev's consultant Stanislav Shatalin and economist Grigoriy Yavlinsky developed a program of privatization called "500 days". Since the state had all the property, and people - all the money, the program envisaged the exchange of one for another. It had to begin with privatization of apartments, small lots, stores, trucks, workshops, and gradually shift to large factories, mines, and oil fields. Had this program been implemented, the state would have liquidated the excess money, normalized finances, and probably would have come out of the crisis without the collapse of the Soviet Union. But the government declined the program and proposed its own plan.

On January 23, 1991 it was announced over the radio in morning news that 50 - and 100-ruble bills were no longer accepted for circulation. All deposits on personal bank accounts were frozen at the same time. People were allowed to exchange cash on hands for new bills within three days and no more than 1,000 rubles per person. The government justified the exchange by allegations that shady businessmen amassed huge amounts of cash in large bills. The reform was confiscatory; it had retired some of the money from circulation, but the confiscated part was not enough for normalization of the economy.

Two months later Mikhail Gorbachev ventured to raise retail prices on essential consumer goods. On April 2, 1991 retail prices in the USSR unexpectedly jumped up by 300% on average (however, they remained under the state control). After the price hike, the frozen personal accounts were partially unblocked and somewhat compensated - the value of deposits was increased by 40%; however, the purchasing power of money had dropped significantly.

For years and years, Soviet people were taking their growing cash accounts for the real wealth. And when Gorbachev sharply raised the prices, millions of people lost their life savings, which they accumulated for retirement, emergency, death in family, etc.

As a result of the price reform, Gorbachev and his government lost people's trust; and the saddest of all was that the reforms brought no visible relief; the store shelves did not become flooded with "concealed" products; the price hike was not sufficient to saturate the market with goods. According to Yegor Gaidar, by the end of next 1991 year Soviet people had accumulated 854 billion rubles, and only 14% of them were secured by goods.[3]

AUGUST 1991 COUP

In 1991, when Gorbachev was on his summer vacation in the Crimea, the top leadership of the Soviet Union declared the state of emergency. August 18-22, 1991 entered into the history of the Soviet Union as days of the "putch" - a military mutiny. The State Emergency Committee and its Chairman Gennady Yanaev proclaimed themselves the top Soviet authority, and formally they violated no laws - Yanaev, as Vice President of the USSR, was the acting Soviet President while Gorbachev vacated in the Crimea. Among the members of the Committee there were the Prime-Minister of the USSR, the Chairman of the KGB, the Minister of the Interior, the Minister of Defense. Strictly speaking, their actions were not a mutiny. But their agenda was a blanket opposition to the Gorbachev's perestroika, to his plans to change the constitution and reform the USSR into the union of independent states. The Committee feared that the upcoming changes would cause a collapse of the USSR. Success of the Committee's coup would mean termination of Gorbachev's reforms and a likely return to the previous order of things.

Sympathies of majority of the Soviet people were neither on the side of Gorbachev, nor on the side of the Committee. Only one top politician decidedly stood up against the Committee; it was Boris Yeltsin, recently elected president of the Russian Federation (one of the fifteen Soviet republics). Yeltsin was supported by Moscow, St. Petersburg, and Sverdlovsk (he was the top communist party executive in Sverdlovsk for a number of years). He and his supporters changed the fate of the country.

Yeltsin had not waged a protracted war of laws, which the Committee would surely have won; he accused Yanaev and other top leaders of the USSR in committing a coup d'état and in the illegal dismissal of President Gorbachev. Yeltsin called for a nationwide strike and arrest of the initiators of the "coup". He declined any compromise with the Committee and pushed its members on the path of power counter play. On August 19, 1991, in the evening news the Soviet central television unexpectedly broadcast Yeltsin's speech at the House of Soviets, the residence of the Supreme Soviet of People's Deputies of the Russian Federation, also called the Russian Parliament. The entire country saw the news. Crowds of Muscovites came to the parliament building to support Yeltsin.

The army that the Committee relied upon surrounded the House of Soviets, but did not storm the main center of resistance, because the Committee did not want to shed blood. Yeltsin, along with his supporters, peacefully entered the parliament building, from where he operated the "headquarters of the revolution". Rather than arresting Yeltsin and his team, the military allowed them to work. On the third day of the coup the army troops retreated.

The main reason why the parliament building was not stormed by the Committee was unwillingness of the coup leaders to start mass slaughter. They chose to surrender to Gorbachev, who, likely not privy to the coup plans, did not spare the coup members and let Yeltsin to imprison them. More than that, Gorbachev gave Yeltsin an opportunity to fully seize power believing that he, as the president of the USSR, would retain his influence anyway. Yeltsin took advantage of the situation for the complete suppression of Gorbachev's authority. Before the putsch, Yeltsin was just the president of one of the fifteen Soviet republics, reporting to Gorbachev. Immediately after the coup, Yeltsin practically deposed Gorbachev: he had issued a decree by which all executive authorities and law enforcement agencies of the USSR passed under jurisdiction of the Russian Republic - under his arm. Enjoying his immense power, Yeltsin did not miss the opportunity to crush the first Soviet President Gorbachev in front of the Congress of People's Deputies of Russia.

What would have happened if the August coup had been successful? Nothing good in the short run, anyway. The country was just a few weeks away from bankruptcy and stopping its debt payments. The Yanaev government would not have received large loans from the western banks. The new authorities would have been forced to further reduce import of grain and other food products, cut livestock numbers, shut down many plants due to the lack of supplies coming from abroad. The Soviet Union would have come back to the planned economy or begun privatization, hoping for the increase in world prices on oil and gas. With some luck we would have obtained that kind of economy we observe now in China. However, the August 1991 coup failed. And people who came to power as a result of the defeat of the State Emergency Committee brought the Soviet Union and then Russia to a collapse.

At the time we spent every spare minute at the TV screens in anticipation of more news. Yeltsin banned the Communist Party of the USSR on the territory of the Russian Federation; this happened in the country that was headed by the Communist Party for over seventy years! All the party's assets had passed to the Councils of People's Deputies of the Russian Federation. Gorbachev was forced to voluntarily resign from the Communist Party leadership and called members of the party's Central Committee to dissolution. Formally, he was still the President of the Soviet Union, but his power was shrinking every day.

After the putsch, watching the collapse of the central government, all Soviet republics declared their independence (despite the results of the All-Union referendum on the future of the USSR, according to which eight of fifteen republics wanted to retain the Soviet Union). The Soviet Union de facto (and soon de jure) ceased to exist. All power in the Russian Federation passed into the hands of Boris Yeltsin.

We experienced mixed feelings in these days. We were against Gorbachev and his government for their failing reforms, but we did not want to return to the old days of total party control of our lives. We tied our hopes for a better life with Yeltsin, perceiving him as an advocate for ordinary people. He accused the party leadership in moral degradation and divergence from their ideological goals. Yeltsin's words were in tune with what we discussed in private conversations. His speeches were plain, and he himself looked like a simple, ordinary man, an unselfish truth-seeker, who said what he thought, no-frills. From being just a popular political figure, Yeltsin quickly turned into a folk hero. But if in August 1991 he had disclosed his plans to dissolve the USSR, he would have lost the people's love. Majority of Soviet people wanted to retain the Union of Soviet Socialist Republics.

Many times Yeltsin publicly promised that he would keep previous standards of living during the transition to the free market economy. He said a catchy phrase: he would lie down under a train in case if he let the price of bread go up. Of course, the price of bread surged, but the phrase has been remembered by many.

Being at the peak of his popularity, Yeltsin declared at the XIX Party Conference (1988) that his goal would be to launch such a mechanism in the party and in the society that would exclude autocrats and their cult and create genuine democracy. Having seized power, Yeltsin quickly became another Russian tyrant, an autocrat, who enjoyed the unlimited power and servility. And Russia slowly but surely began to slide into the bygone era of Tsars, and the poverty circa 1989 started looking like prosperity to many people ten years later.

On December 8, 1991, at the hunting farm for the top Soviet executives in the Belorussian National Park, Boris Yeltsin (leader of Russia), Leonid Kravchuk (leader of Ukraine) and Stanislav Shushkievich (leader of Belarus) gathered to sign the Belavezha Accords, which announced the dissolution of the Soviet Union as a subject of international law. Formally, the USSR was founded in 1922 by four republics: the Russian Federation, Ukraine, Belarus, and Transcaucasia. Transcaucasia did not exist anymore, so the other three sister republics seemed to have the right to declare the Union abolished.

Twenty years later, Yegor Ligachev, the former Secretary of the Central Committee of the USSR Communist Party, gave an interview to the newspaper Komsomolskaya Pravda:

> People always ask me: who was the major figure in the collapse of the Soviet Union, who was to blame for all the ills that hit the people with terrible force? Time has given the answer to this difficult question: Gorbachev. And the follower of Gorbachev's deed Boris Yeltsin, who had brought citizens of the richest with natural resources country to poverty. He played this role till the

end. At the XIX Party Conference in 1988 I said: 'Boris, you're wrong! You have the energy, but your energy is destructive, not constructive.' The prediction proved correct. I would have been happy if I had made a mistake. [4]

For Russia, geographical consequences of the Belavezha Accords were disastrous. Russian boundaries have shrunk to the borders of 1613 year. With a stroke of a pen Yeltsin had written off about fifty million people who viewed Russian as their native language. [5]

On December 25, 1991 Gorbachev had to resign from the presidency of the Soviet Union. On the same day Boris Yeltsin officially obtained full presidential power in Russia, a residence in the Kremlin, and the so-called nuclear suitcase.

Boris Yeltsin gathered a new Russian government from representatives of intellectual environment - researchers and professors. The government was run by Yegor Gaidar, an economist-theoretician, former head of the economic department of the top political journal in the Soviet Union - The Communist. And this government had to deal with the urgent task of saving the country. Yeltsin knew little beyond the politics, but economist Gaidar frantically believed in the free market ability to fix any ills of the Russian economy and started his term with full liberalization of prices. This measure, according to Gaidar, was to encourage farmers to sell food products and businesses - to saturate internal market with goods.

In December 1991 our new state - the Russian Federation - experienced devastation, chaos, paralysis of agriculture and manufacturing, total confusion and lack of everything. In most regions residents were supplied with no more than 1 kg of sugar, 0.5 kg of meat products (with bones), 0.2 kg of butter per person per month (by coupon system). On January 2, 1992 all businesses and retailers were permitted to set their own prices for goods; any import restrictions were abolished. From that day onward anyone could sell anything, anywhere, at any price and in any quantities (except narcotics etc.) - Russia has switched to the free market economy.

On the first business day of 1992, retail prices soared to the sky. There were products on the shelves we had not seen for decades. Now we could stare at them but could not buy because of the numbers on the price tags. We did not believe that those price levels were sustainable. Alas, by the end of 1992 they grew even higher: annual price hike on eggs was 1900%, on bread - 4300%, on milk - 4800%, on tobacco - 3600%, on soap and shampoo - 3100%, to take a few.[5, 6] Meanwhile the wages grew just slightly. It was a terrible blow to us. Retail prices in the USSR had been constant for decades: a loaf of white bread cost 0.2 rubles, a liter of milk - about 0.2 rubles, a glass of a non-alcoholic drink - 0.03 rubles, a public transit pass - 0.03-0.06 rubles, an airplane ticket for a roundtrip Siberia-Moscow about 50 rubles (with average salary being about 200 rubles per month in 1985[1]). The retail prices had been factory-stamped on all the goods. To sell something for a higher price than the one set by the state was a criminal offence. Those times were now gone forever.

Yegor Gaidar had reached his goal - he had filled the stores with goods, solved the problem of deficit, and defeated the ubiquitous queues. However, another, far more serious problem popped up: the new retail prices were utterly high. Gaidar did not attempt to curb monopolies that Russia inherited from the Soviet economy, and these monopolies brazenly set pricing policies the way they wanted, not being restricted by any competition. If competitors did show up, they were eliminated by shooting off or by some other ways of suppression. Yes, there was food in stores, but we had no money. That's when we started seeing ragged and impoverished people rummaging garbage bins for food - these were mostly retirees who lost their savings.

At the same time, Gaidar fought inflation via cuts in budget spending by orders of magnitude and via reduced printing of money ("shock therapy"); these measures helped him to execute the state budget of the first quarter of 1992 without deficit. Stabilization - limiting the state budget's deficit - was a precondition for lending money, put forward by the International Monetary Fund and the World Bank. The main objective of the measures announced in Russia, as British the Guardian wrote at the time, was to butter up the IMF to receive substantial financial assistance from the West. Western experts (e.g. from the Cato Institute in Washington, DC) feared that pressure from Russian people, unhappy with the decline in their living standards, will not let Gaidar maintain his tough financial policy. Also, the experts did not like the fact that the Central Bank of Russia was under control of the Supreme Soviet of the People's Deputies (the legislative branch of power), but not under the government (the executive branch of power). The leadership of the Central Bank of Russia believed that the Gaidar's shock therapy would lead to the collapse of the financial system, and the result would be a paralysis of the economy as a whole. Future developments showed that their concerns were justified. Disagreements between the Supreme Soviet and the Gaidar government over the "shock therapy" began to accumulate from that time onward and culminated in the civil war in October of 1993.

Meanwhile, due to the hike in prices and limited money supply, Russian businesses of non-primary sectors were left virtually without any working capital, which caused an acute crisis of mutual non-payments between enterprises. Because of the widespread non-payments, businesses did not have funds to pay wages to their employees. Providers of utilities were about to stop their services: water and electricity supply, transportation, etc. We received our salaries with 6-9 months' delay, and our savings had been devaluated and frozen. And the country got swept by the shaft of street and organized crime.

In the province, majority of people survived by working on three-four jobs at the same time. We heard of instantly made fortunes, saw movies and TV shows about new Russian oligarchs squandering millions of dollars on luxury items, and understood that the same mechanisms that had enriched a narrow group of people caused mass impoverishment of all the other Russians.

The Gaidar's full liberalization of prices completely changed the economic landscape in Russia: the golden times for cooperatives were gone. Directors of state enterprises received total freedom in setting prices and selling their goods whomever and wherever they wanted. A special decree permitted anybody, who leased a state plant, supplied it with raw materials, and paid wages to its employees, to own the products of this plant and do with them whatever the new managers wanted. Earlier, the government had annulled the monopoly on foreign trade. Liberalization of foreign trade along with liberalization of internal prices was supposed to quickly equalize the world and the domestic prices on goods, especially on petroleum products and industrial metals. The price of these commodities on the world market was much higher, and the domestic prices began to grow. However, the establishment of equilibrium after the liberalization took considerable time for such a big country as Russia with its weak ties between regions - about two years. In the meantime, revenue from the price differential for primary resources went into the pockets of private firms. Although these revenues had disappeared with time (when the domestic prices approached the levels of the world ones), they were so high in the initial period that instantly enriched a small group of individuals - those who were in the right place at the right time.

The internal price hike on the mineral resources caused collapse of the processing and manufacturing industries in Russia. In the Soviet economy, low cost of crude and energy offset the lack of technological advancement and efficiency in many industries, thus helping them to stay afloat. The rising prices on raw materials and energy dramatically complicated the situation in the processing and manufacturing sectors, enormously increasing their cost of production. Some of them (light industry, agriculture, housing, and utilities) became chronically unprofitable soon.

In addition, sales of crude at negligible export tariffs with weak customs controls, providing profits of thousand percents, made pointless investing in the production and development of technology, resulting in total decline of the Russian industry and growth of corruption and crime.

Directors of enterprises in resource industry, having opened offshore trading companies, started selling their products, but did not return revenue back to Russia, because they did not own their enterprises and were not interested in re-investing profits into their businesses. Their production and employees suffered from non-payments. "It's every man for himself," was the main motto at the time. The state and the majority of population impoverished, for the government, having lost its major source of income, could not pay pensions and federal workers' wages, fund military, medicine, education and culture.

By the end of 1992, differentiation of citizens to the rich and the poor had increased dramatically; 44% of the population lived below the poverty line. The Russian society plunged into the unprecedented destitution.

That's when we began pondering about what we have lost and gained.

Socialism provided everyone with a job in favorite profession. Socialism meant guaranteed free education of your choice, if you had adequate abilities and aptitude, and absolutely free of charge medical care. Socialism liberated us from worrying about the future: under any circumstances we would have a job and bread on the table, and guaranteed decent pension upon retirement. Of course, socialistic boons were not distributed evenly: some people vacated in resorts more often than others, their children went to better summer camps etc. All socialistic advantages we took for granted and focused only on its shortcomings, like inequalities in the distribution of perks, low wages, deficit of goods. In the socialist Soviet society, a highly skilled worker did not receive compensation for his labor as high as his colleague in similar profession in the western countries and had a limited choice of goods to buy, but the socialist system did not push people to work hard and satisfied all basic needs of its citizens. Under the Soviet socialism it was difficult to shutdown unprofitable enterprises and intensify work - it could lead to unemployment. For a long time, until mid 1980s, the Soviet socialist economy did not eliminate economically unprofitable enterprises and had zero unemployment rates; the Soviets were able to concentrate a lot of efforts and resources on solving historically important tasks, such as space exploration and militarization of the country. In the Brezhnev years, the Soviet society was the paradise on earth in comparison to the western countries, but we did not know that - we came to recognition of that three decades later.

The shortcomings of the socialism were overlapped by its enormous advantages, but we did not understand that the perks we enjoyed was a result of the developed socialism; we thought that any modern society provided its members with the same; we believed that the social benefits would surely remain after the Gorbachev's and Yeltsin's reforms. We were wrong. The standards of living in the 1990s were horrendously worse than the ones in 1980s.

Alexandr Zinoviev, a known anti-Soviet dissident in the past, became an advocate of communism in 1990s. In his books he noted that Soviet people had minimum of everything, but minimum guaranteed, something as natural and unshakeable as access to air and water. The Soviet people of older generation, who used to live under the socialism, now realized that attempting to follow the path of the West they lost more than they gained.

We were deceived: we had voted neither for the murderous "liberalization" of prices, nor for the uncontrolled power of monopolies, nor for the collapse and looting of the state, but for the hope for a better life.[8]

PRIVATIZATION

For us, ordinary people, life was changing at a staggering pace. The confiscatory monetary reform, the soaring prices, the Gaidar's shock therapy devalued our life savings. And then the government started privatization exactly when people were left with nothing in their pockets.

In summer of 1992, President Yeltsin said that the country needed millions of owners rather than a handful of millionaires, in the new economy, everyone would have an equal opportunity, and a privatization voucher would be a ticket to it. A voucher was each citizen's share in the property of the former Soviet Union - an impersonal check with face value of 10,000 rubles.

Yeltsin signed a decree on the voucher privatization in August of 1992 and asked Anatoly Chubais to lead the process. In the course of the privatization, the vouchers were distributed to all citizens, one per person. Large enterprises were corporatized for the privatization, and their shares were partly sold at the voucher auctions, partly reserved for the state, and partly distributed among employees of those enterprises. The former state monopolies became the private ones, but the new collective owners turned to be mediocre businessmen, aimed at achieving personal short-term gains. And in the next few years a re-privatization occurred: a small group of wealthy people acquired businesses and properties via buying up shares and vouchers, as well as via raider seizures. That's when the actual private companies were formed.[2]

If ordinary citizens did not want to invest their vouchers in the enterprise of which they were employees (especially when they saw its nearing bankruptcy), they had a few more options: just sell them for cash, or put their vouchers in mutual voucher investment funds. By mid-1994, there were 662 mutual voucher funds, and they had accumulated 45 million vouchers (32% of the total vouchers issued). The fund managers had purchased approximately 10% of shares of the privatized enterprises. Then the vast majority of the funds sold these shares at a very low cost to the most influential groups (often from organized crime), filed for bankruptcy, and liquidated themselves. That is, 45 million people, who trusted the voucher funds, did not receive anything for their shares of the Soviet property. Not better off were people who sold their vouchers for cash or bought shares of their companies of which they were employees. Anatoly Chubais promised that the purchasing power of one voucher would be equal to the cost of two new "Volga" automobiles (the best Soviet passenger car), but the actual market value of a voucher turned out to be negligible; in winter of 1992-93 it was roughly equal to two bottles of vodka.

At the time, a good choice was to buy shares of primary resource companies such as Gazprom. Gazprom owned up to a third of global gas resources; it was the sole gas supplier to the former Soviet Union and the major gas supplier to the Western Europe, the richest company in Russia and maybe in the whole world. Had Gazprom been appraised by the western economists, only its gas resources would have been worth on the market between 300 and 700 billion dollars. Many people wanted to buy shares of Gazprom. Analyst Alexei Peshkov spent a lot of time untangling complex privatization schemes of Gazprom. The results of his research are below.

At the time of privatization, all shares of Gazprom were valued at $ 47,000,000 USD; that's how much 10,000 gas and oil wells, 154 gas treatment plants, six plants for gas and oil processing, 155,000 km of gas pipelines and its laterals, 253 compressor stations with total capacity of more than 42 million kilowatts, 22 underground gas storage facilities and 3,583 gas distribution stations were estimated to cost. Gazprom had considerable assets "blurred" in subsidiaries, too.

The state gas giant had issued 237 Mln shares, 40% of which the government reserved for itself.

The Gazprom shares were distributed via two ways: 1) 15% of the shares were offered to the employees of Gazprom, half of the shares they could buy for cash, and half - for the vouchers; and 2) the remainder of shares (more than 100 Mln) could be acquired via voucher auctions. At the auctions Gazprom was selling his shares exclusively for the vouchers, and it collected 8.3 million vouchers. So one voucher was supposed to buy several Gazprom shares. In fact, those who were lucky to buy them received less than one share per voucher! There were no other, non-voucher auctions or sales till the first gathering of Gazprom shareholders on May 31, 1995.

Yeltsin's privatization decree never called for discrimination on the basis of residency. But Chubais allowed sales of Gazprom shares only in certain regions, which, in fact, was that same discrimination. In order to divide the voucher holders into "us" and "them", it was decided to hold the auctions not all over Russia, but in the regions where there was a Gazprom enterprise. And only citizens with passports registered in those areas were allowed to participate in the Gazprom auctions. The general public did not know of this, because no one warned us about the importance of passport registration in certain regions for purchase of the Gazprom shares. Thus the overwhelming majority of Russian citizens had no right to take part in the Gazprom auctions.

Making privatization results even more unfair, Chubais and his managers allocated different number of shares to the areas where the Gazprom held his auctions. The regions, where more vouchers had been collected, received fewer shares (especially large cities like Moscow). Some other regions, where the population density and income per capita were very low and only minimum of vouchers had been gathered, received many times more shares than Moscow. One example: population of the entire Tyumen region was about 3 million people. Residents of this area bought nearly 17 million shares, while in Moscow with 8 million residents Gazprom sold only 40,000 shares. In Yamal-Nenets district - a part of the Tyumen region - Gazprom sold additional 13 million shares. In total, 30 Mln shares were sold in the region with 3 Mln population. Maybe it was done with good intentions to provide better opportunities for the poor local population. But good intentions paved road to hell. The poor Tyumen residents could not compete at the auctions with emissaries of people in power who provided their agents with money and local registration. These large regional Gazprom shareholders from the voucher auctions all happened to be from Moscow, after all.

The roguery with the Gazprom shares did not end after the voucher auctions. Too many shares happened to be in the "wrong hands". In 1996, the Gazprom shares were posted for trading on stock market. At the time, the stock market prices of most Russian companies were rapidly growing, but Gazprom did not pay any dividends and artificially slowed down the growth of its stock. This forced many shareholders to sell its Gazprom stock for next to nothing and invest in other companies. Number of Gazprom shareholders fell by two-thirds by 1998. That's when, after buying up large blocks of shares by its subsidiaries, the company announced increase in the nominal value of its shares by 500 times, that is by 50,000%.[10] That's how the most profitable state assets were privatized.

Some of the best Russian companies were bought out by their directors of the Soviet era. Typically, these were people who used to secretly siphon money from the businesses they managed and now with that money they were able to buy vouchers to bid in the primary auction or buy back shares from their employees in the secondary market. Since payment of wages was often delayed by half a year or longer, their workers were happy to sell their vouchers or shares for cash.

Within the next two years the government managed to sell domestically half of the state property at enormous, unimaginable loss. Sea ports with their entire infrastructure and ships had been sold for the price of an old barge. Solid businesses producing exportable commodities were sold for a sum equal to their monthly profit. The legendary "UralMash", a pride of the Urals industry and the center of the global heavy machinery (34,000 workers), was bought by Kaha Bendukidze, a microbiologist from Georgia, for two car trunks stuffed with vouchers, which were worth approximately $450,000. The famous Chelyabinsk Tractor Plant was sold for $ 2,200,000 USD. The legendary automotive plant "GAZ" with 140,000 employees - for $ 25,000,000 USD.[11] The selling prices were low because only a handful of people had cash to buy up vouchers to participate in the auctions - they were mostly the ones who made fortunes trading primary resources to foreign buyers.

As economists say now, the Russian industrial giants in strategic sectors such as oil and gas, metals, aluminum, space exploration should have become the state corporations. Instead, Chubais had sold off the largest and most profitable enterprises to private investors, who often were connected with criminals.

Pavel Voshchanov, the former press secretary of President Boris Yeltsin, recalled that in early 1990s the top Russian leaders had planned that the majority of the state assets would go to the previous "elite" - the higher rank party officials and top Soviet managers, and the privatization would progress under the strict government control.[12] In other words, from the beginning the authorities did not anticipate real participation of the population in the privatization, but they underestimated the extent of the accumulated criminal money; these amounts happened to be quite comparable with the financial capabilities of the previous elite. Therefore, from the start, there were two groups of buyers: from "the top" and from "the bottom", and fierce competition between them resulted in gang wars and shoot off of new businessmen and bankers.

Majority of the population was plunged into dire poverty, which was justified by the government as an unavoidable stage in the initial accumulation of capitals. A small group had really made fortunes in a matter of days, while the Russian industry as a whole was on a sharp and steady decline. Spread of rumors about impending food shortage forced millions of people to grow potato and vegetables in their garden plots; the country returned to the medieval subsistence farming, and Chubais and Gaidar were proud that they avoided mass starvation.

In 1993, the government hit us with another confiscatory monetary reform. People were allowed to exchange up to one hundred thousand rubles but only in the locality where they were registered as residents. The reform was carried out during the vacation season, when most people were away from their homes. The territorial restriction for the money exchange intended to combat the influx of currency banknotes from the former Soviet republics. Many people could not return to their homes in time for the exchange, so

27

they lost their savings again.

Demographic statistics of the first years of the Yeltsin era trumpeted disaster the world history had not known in the peacetime. From 1990 to 1994 the male mortality rate soared by 53%, the female mortality - by 27%. In 1990, male life expectancy was 64 years; by 1994 it reduced to 58 years. For the first time after the Second World War, the Russian population began to decline. According to the RosStat, every year until the end of Yeltsin's presidency Russia was losing about one million people.[2, 12] In the peacetime such declines were observed only after catastrophic epidemics or famine.

CRIMINALIZATION OF RUSSIA

To the sharp decline in living standards, non-payment of wages, bankruptcy of almost all enterprises of non-primary sectors the population responded with the growth of the shadow economy, corruption, and crime.

The law enforcement virtually vanished; the state did not protect people anymore; crimes of all kinds blossomed; and we fell under authority of gangs. Previous system of spiritual and moral values collapsed. In short, we were in the situation of lawlessness. Lucky new owners of the former Soviet enterprises became wealthy overnight. They were buying luxury foreign cars and exquisite clothes, building themselves castles in the suburbs... Very soon they were visited by local crime bosses, who had armies of bandits for racketeering, exactly like in *Once Upon a Time in America*. In theory, liberalization of economy should have resulted in conversion of the shady operations into the legitimate business, but the opposite occurred: the black market sucked in the new businesses.

Hearing about enormous profits of businessmen, officials of the state apparatus demanded their share of cash flow, and the commercial success turned out to be dependent upon political connections. Complex and confusing tax code hampered operations of businesses; majority of them carried two sets of accounting books. There was no effective legal system; contracts were not executed as they were supposed to, and it was impossible to collect debts.

The state, implementing privatization, did not provide safeguards for businesses. In developed countries businesses could apply to different dispute resolution services, but in Russia such arbitration did not work. Even if you won your case in the court, you weren't able to collect debts. Criminal gangs actively took over empty niche of the business arbitration, performing its functions and knocking out money from debtors.

In 1990s, more than 90 percent of the private businesses in Russia had connections with gangsters and thieves in one way or another, and every businessman had personal security guards. Majority of the security firms were semi-criminal structures.[14]

In 1990s, the total number of "private security guards" in Russia was estimated at 800,000 people, and these were highly trained professionals: past Soviet athletes, officers of the special forces, KGB and militsiya (police) officers who lost their state jobs.[5, 14] Government drastically cut budget expenses, and these professionals, trained to kill, had nowhere to go other than to the security agencies or to the criminal gangs (one did not exclude the other).

Banks and export industries were a tasty morsel for the organized crime. In 1993, directors of privatized oil refineries, aluminum smelters, logging companies were being shot one by one. Murders became the primary way to deal with competitors. Rather than settling their differences through mediation or in court, businessmen hired professional killers and solved their problems with firearms. There were hundreds of skirmishes in Moscow, often taking place in the middle of the day. Competitors were shot with pistols, machine guns, grenade launchers, bombs hid under the cars. From 1989 to 1993, number of murders in Moscow increased by 800%.[2, 14] Although the police was unable to stop the violence, many police officers died fighting with criminals.

Situation with the judicial system was even worse than with the law enforcement. Russia had no judges who were experts on organized crime; the law did not allow culprits to enter a plea agreement; there was neither witness protection program nor anything similar to RICO Act. Moreover, Russian judges had reputation of supple - they used to comply with demands of the Soviet authorities; they could be manipulated with bribes or threats. The police complained: even if they managed to arrest the most notorious villains, key witnesses usually abandoned their testimonies in court, and the judges closed the case.

Alexei Ivanov provided a classic example of a criminal deceit in his book *Ordered Crimes: Murders, Thefts, Robberies*.[15] A gangster's company through a legitimate representative takes a loan, secured by a contract - for example, for purchase of sausages from Estonia. The contract is a fake. The money are converted into foreign currency and sent to Estonia, usually through a long chain of intermediaries. When the money is deposited in a western bank, it remains to shoot the Russian banker who gave the loan in order to clean up the traces.

Russian gangsters thrived, becoming not only wealthy but also famous; their feats were spotlighted by newspapers and TVs; their photos in the company of ministers and mayors of major cities appeared everywhere. The general public began buying dictionaries of prison slang and novels about exploits of criminal heroes; political analysts investigated the gangsters' world. In the early 1990s our state created "greenhouse" conditions for the organized crime - they were buying businesses, gaining political connections, and strengthening their economic and financial capacity.

Mikhail Weller said in his book *The Great Last Chance*: if export of crude and import of consumer goods is more profitable than their production, if it is more profitable to sell imported cars than develop competitive domestic ones, if to take and give bribes is more profitable than to live honestly, then the market becomes destructive, eradicating domestic industry along with ideology and morality. If I can buy for a ruble and re-sell for a million, I will not work. If I can sell oil for a billion of dollars without spending a penny for exploration, equipment replacement, etc., I won't invest in technology and development. Russian market has inevitably acquired the destructive character and knocked out of the manufacturing industry the most energetic, intelligent, and adventurous managers pushing them into the export of crude, crime, politics, emigration.[16]

It took almost twenty years for the free market economy in Russia to approach the GDP of 1990 year, when Russia had socialistic economy and was a part of the USSR. In 1985-1990, GDP of the Russian Federation was 60% of the GDP of the Soviet Union, according to the CIA estimations in

The World Fact book and Statistical Abstract of the United States).[17]

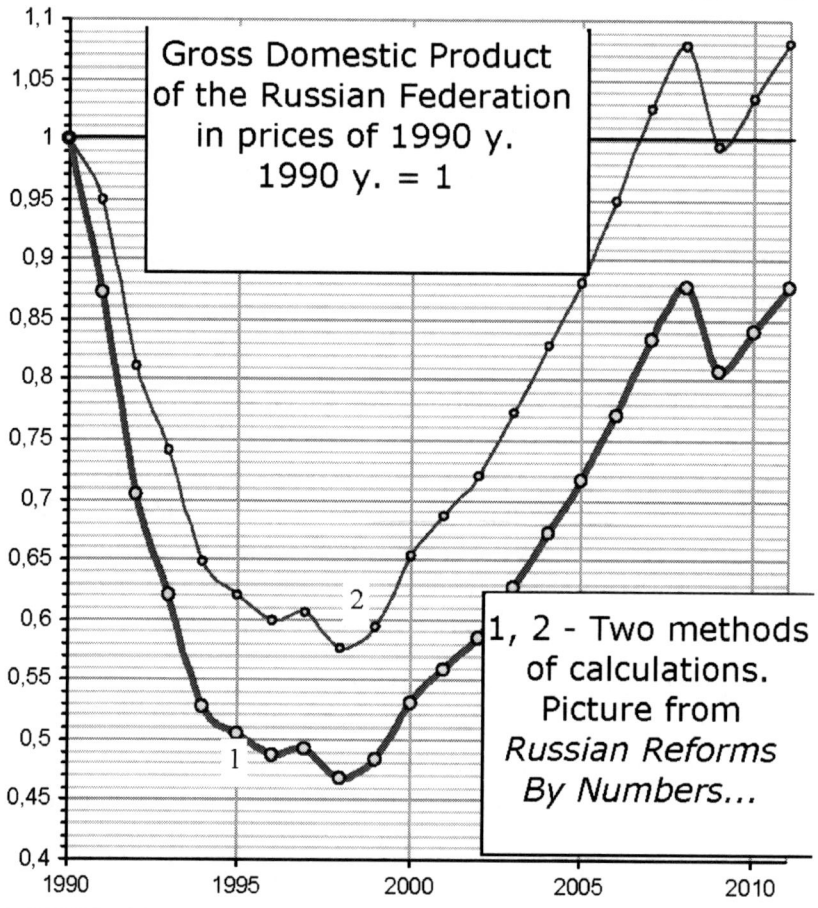

Picture 1. Gross Domestic Product of the Russian Federation in 1990-2010

In 1992 inflation in Russia reached 2609%. As a result of the hyper-inflation, 100 billion rubles of monetary deposits on personal accounts of the Russian people terribly depreciated, and the population viewed it as a direct rip-off by the state. Real income per capita in 1992 dropped almost two-fold on average in comparison with 1991.[17, 18]

CRISIS OF POWER

The shock therapy of 1992 made those of us, who previously worshiped Yeltsin, hate him. Problems were rolling across the country as a snowball. The promised economic miracle was not happening. The Supreme Soviet of the Russian Federation - a permanent Parliament, elected by the Congress of People's Deputies and headed by Ruslan Khasbulatov, a puppet of Yeltsin in 1991, began to oppose him. Leaving the Parliament to become the President of Russia, Yeltsin nominated Ruslan Khasbulatov for the vacant post of its Speaker, the Chairman of the Supreme Soviet. Ruslan Khasbulatov was a doctor of economic science and a graduate of the top Soviet university; he owed his political career to Yeltsin, but soon he began gradually turning from his ally into the worst Yeltsin's enemy.

Up until 1989, the Supreme Soviet of the Russian Federation was the highest power, competent to decide literally any question allotted to the authority of the Russian Federation. From December 15, 1990 to December 9, 1992, the competences of the parliament were repeatedly refined due to the collapse of the Soviet Union and the ongoing constitutional reform in the country. However, despite all the 1991-1992 constitutional amendments proclaiming separation of legislative and executive powers, the parliament still possessed real power: it could stop privatization of the state assets (or just transfer them to the emerging oligarchy for free); it could dismiss from the post any minister and initiate legal proceedings against him; it could announce impeachment of the president and request early elections, etc. The first democratic parliament had a lot of shortcomings and deficiencies in the work, its deputies had no developed political culture and professionalism, but it was indeed an independent authority, and there was no other way to eliminate it except by resorting to brutal force. The confrontation of the legislative (parliament) and executive (president) power branches in Russia ended exactly in that.

When the Gaidar government began its reforms, Ruslan Khasbulatov, a known economist perfectly versed in economics problems (unlike Yeltsin), argued that there was no need to hurry up so feverishly, that Gaidar's expectations were overly optimistic. Khasbulatov did not hide his emotions, believing that he could help Yeltsin to correct the government's course. But the president did not appreciate the parliament's intervention, and step by step the parliament and the president became opposed to each other.

Vice President Alexandr Rutskoi, an air force colonel, set off to Siberia for an official visit at the end of 1991. What he had seen there shocked him to the core. People were barely surviving because payments of salaries and pensions were delayed for 6-9 months, many municipalities did not provide heat and electricity for housing because of lack of money in the regional budgets. Rutskoi said harsh words about the Gaidar government: "Boys in pink panties." The expression was so well-aimed that permanently entered the political lexicon denoting arrival to the political Olympus of the "parquet theorists" - people with no practical and managerial experience. The president was instantly reported that Rutskoi attacked his henchmen and, therefore, him, too.

The Yeltsin associates passed Khasbulatov's and Rutskoi's talks to Yeltsin, often shifting accents and exaggerating. These seeds of hostility were falling on fertile ground. Every time, having heard a new batch of gossips, Yeltsin fell into a rage and clenched his fists angrily. Roughly the same occurred to Rutskoi and Khasbulatov, when similar schemers set them up against Yeltsin. Khasbulatov repeatedly phoned Yeltsin, trying to smooth some of the problems in direct conversation with the president, but Yeltsin refused to talk to him.

In December of 1992, at the Seventh Congress of People's Deputies, Ruslan Khasbulatov attempted to amend the Constitution, aiming to limit the presidential power and give the parliament the right to form the government: he was short of four (only!) votes to adopt the amendment. At the Congress, the deputies attested the work of the government as unsatisfactory. Yeltsin was forced to negotiate with the Supreme Soviet regarding the candidature of a new prime-minister. The president offered the parliament a compromise: he would remove Gaidar, hated by people, and offer the parliament three other candidates for a prime-minister post, but in exchange the parliament would conduct a referendum, letting people decide the future development of Russia.

Ultimately, the parliament chose Victor Chernomyrdin as the new prime minister; Chernomyrdin was the former Minister of Gas Industry and one of the top party officials. Chernomyrdin brought along a new team of seasoned managers, proudly calling themselves "industrialists" and "statesmen". But the new team changed little in the governance of the country.

THE RUSSIAN PARLIAMENT IS DEFEATED

With resignation of Gaidar from the post of the prime-minister in December of 1992, hostility between the parliament and the president did not end; on the contrary, it gained momentum. The Eighth Congress of the People's Deputies, which opened on Mar 10, 1993, was marked by a scandal. The deputies proposed to impeach Yeltsin; in response, the president defiantly left the chamber, calling on his supporters-deputies to join him. But he was followed by a very few, and it was a blow to his self-esteem. However, the impeachment did not go through; only 617 deputies out of 1033 had voted for it, while minimally 689 votes were needed. The Congress set the All-Russian Referendum for April 25, 1993, honoring the previous agreement between the parliament and the president.

After the obstruction Yeltsin received at the Eighth Congress on March 20, 1993, he suddenly gave a speech to the nation on television: he suspended the work of the parliament and introduced a special order of governance in the country. Yeltsin's announcement resembled very much actions of the State Emergency Committee in August of 1991, and the Constitutional Court declared it invalid. On March 26, 1993 Ruslan Khasbulatov hastily convened the Ninth Extraordinary Congress, specifically to vote on the impeachment of the president. Had the impeachment been approved by the people's deputies, Alexandr Rutskoi, then current vice president, would have become the acting president of Russia. And again the parliament was short of a few votes to reach the 689 vote minimum for the impeachment. Soon the Supreme Soviet realized that the decree Yeltsin signed on March contained no declarations about dissolution of the parliament. The Yeltsin's televised address was probably a provocation, prepared by some of Yeltsin's associates.

Meanwhile the country held the referendum, the outcome of which could decide the fate of the president and the parliament. People had to answer four questions: 1) whether they trusted Yeltsin, 2) and his economic politics, 3) whether they wanted the pre-term presidential elections or 4) the pre-term parliament elections. The people's deputies were confident that the country would not support Yeltsin and his reforms. Contrary to their expectations, majority of Russians still believed the president, despite the shock therapy of his government, maybe because there were no political leaders of comparable caliber in the opposition camp. Of the people who came to the polls, 58.7% voted for Yeltsin and 53.0% - in favor of his economic reforms; they neither wanted the pre-term presidential election, nor the early parliament election. In short, people voted for Yeltsin to stay and for the parliament to stay. As to the shock therapy, everybody hoped that we had hit the bottom already, and now turning back would not make any sense; we believed that our life would only become better from now on. Time proved us wrong.

Subsequent events of September and October of 1993 - an armed confrontation between the Supreme Soviet and the president - had long remained a mystery to me. Mass media reported that Yeltsin dissolved the parliament, suspended activity of opposition, banned distribution of the opposition's newspapers and magazines, and planned to amend the constitution. I saw in the news tanks firing at the people's deputies in the Moscow core; read about hundreds of victims and atrocities of "red-brown bandits", and heard about arrests of "rebels" (the "rebels" were the legitimately elected members of the parliament). But only many years later, from memoirs of participants of the events, interviews with prosecutors-investigators, research papers of historians and political analysts I grasped the entire picture. Shameful to admit, I even did not know that my home region - Novosibirsk - strongly opposed Yeltsin in October of 1993.

Sergey Pykhtin, a philosopher, writer, and one of the founders of the International Congress of Russian Communities, called the October 1993 mutiny a coup of the executive power against the core institutions of the state - the Parliament and the Constitutional Court.[19]

Judge for yourself.

On September 21, 1993, Yeltsin issued the decree 1400 *On the Phased Constitutional Reform in the Russian Federation*, by which he abolished the constitution that was in effect at the time, dissolved the parliament (thus grossly violating the constitutional law), and appointed on December 12, 1993 the pre-term elections of a new parliament and voting for the new constitution. He claimed that the parliament violated the will of the Russian people, who expressed support to Yeltsin on the referendum of April 25, 1993; thus, the parliament opposed itself to the decisions of the All-Russian Referendum, which possessed the supreme legal power. In fact, the April 25 referendum was just a poll, by which the people of Russia demonstrated that they wanted neither the pre-term presidential elections, nor the pre-term parliamentary elections.

The president suggested the people's deputies to return to the institutions where they had worked before becoming the parliament members and to take part in the December elections to the new legislature. Half an hour after the Yeltsin's speech, Vladimir Shumeyko, the vice premier minister of the Yeltsin government announced that the president did not plan to use force or cut off power and heating of the parliament building. Defense Minister Pavel Grachev declared that the armed forces would never act against their own people. However, the government was readying for the worst: a few days before the Yeltsin's announcement of the decree 1400, employees of the military ministries along with the presidential security "suddenly" received 80% salary raise.[20] Based on their past bitter experience, the officers suspected that soon they would be sent into combat. Obviously, the president did not sign the decree "spontaneously", as if offended by Khasbulatov's rudeness, as some newspapers suggested.

On the same day when Yeltsin signed the decree 1400, Ruslan Khasbulatov convened an emergency meeting of the Presidium of the Supreme Soviet, where he warned that the state was in a critical situation and "any events are possible". The Supreme Soviet refused to obey the decree and qualified the president's actions as a coup d'état. Also, the Supreme Soviet decided to convene the Tenth Extraordinary Congress of People's Deputies.

A couple of hours after the Khasbulatov's speech, Gaidar, the former Yeltsin's prime minister, held a meeting with members of the government, where they developed a plan of priority actions for the implementation of the decree 1400, which included cutting off the direct TV translations from the parliament meetings and cordoning off of the parliament building under the pretence of protecting Muscovites from the "armed militants" holed up in the parliament. Soon, the parliament was disconnected from all utilities including communications, power, water, and sewer and cordoned off by a continuous ring of watering machines and a barrage of Bruno wires, as well as by troops of the Interior Ministry and the riot police, who were armed with machine guns, batons, special gas "bird cherry", and had at their disposal the armored personnel carriers (APCs) and water-jet units. They blocked the passage of people, vehicles (including emergency vehicles), delivery of food and first-aid drugs into the cordoned area.

Picture 2. The cordon around the parliament building (by unknown author, from http://psi-overlord.livejournal.com/1271522.html)

The Constitutional Court of the Russian Federation at its extraordinary night session on September 21-22, 1993 came to the conclusion that the presidential decree 1400 had violated twelve provisions of the Russian Constitution and justified the dismissal of Yeltsin from the presidential office. The defense of the parliament building was headed by Vice President Alexandr Rutskoi, Chairman of the Supreme Soviet Ruslan Khasbulatov, and Generals Vladislav Achalov and Albert Makashov.

On September 23, 1993, Valentin Stepankov, the Prosecutor General of the Russian Federation, held a speech at the meeting of the Supreme Soviet; he found Yeltsin's actions unconstitutional and called on both sides to resolve the conflict peacefully by political means.

The Tenth Extraordinary Congress of the People's Deputies started its work on September 25, 1993. There were up to 2,000 people inside the cordon, 689 of them were the people's deputies (628 were needed for the quorum). The Congress approved the decision of the Supreme Soviet to terminate the presidency of Yeltsin and pass it to Vice President Rutskoi. The Yeltsin's decree 1400 was declared to be a coup d'état. The Congress set for March, 1994 both the pre-term presidential and the pre-term parliament elections, acting more fairly than Yeltsin, who wanted only re-election of the parliament in December of 1993.[21]

Yeltsin's representatives met with Vice President Rutskoi and asked him to leave the building and do everything possible for self-dissolution of the Supreme Soviet and the Congress of People's Deputies, promising forgiveness and gratitude for that. Rutskoi refused this offer. The country was dragged in the situation with two presidents and two sets of power ministers, typical for the time of a civil war. The disconnected utilities in the parliament building, the barbed wire cordons, and the police barriers made the deputies look heroes in the national consciousness.

Regional Soviets of the People's Deputies in provinces along with the Moscow Soviet of the People's Deputies fully supported the Supreme Soviet - the Parliament. Heads of seventeen regions of the Urals, Siberia, and the Far East urgently convened a meeting in Novosibirsk and declared that if the decree 1400 and all the documents that followed from it were not cancelled by both sides prior to October 3rd, if normal conditions for the deputies' work were not provided, and if simultaneous pre-term elections of the president and the people's deputies were not set, the assembly of the seventeen regions would adopt the following measures:

- An Extraordinary Congress of the People's Deputies will be held in one of the regional centers in Siberia;

- Tax payments to the capital will be terminated;

- Export of oil, coal, and wood would be stopped;

- Railroad service would be terminated [it was a threat to block the Trans-Siberian railroad artery];

- A regional referendum on the separation of the Siberian Republic from the Russian Federation would be held...

The Novosibirsk police announced that they ceased to obey to the Interior Ministry's orders and would be reporting to the local Council of the People's Deputies.

The All-Siberian Meeting put forward an ultimatum to Yeltsin, demanding to take off the blockade of the parliament and begin negotiations with the Supreme Soviet. Yeltsin failed to dislodge "rebel" Novosibirsk Governor Vitaly Mukha, who was supported by local political parties, businesses, and by the Novosibirsk police department.[20, 22]

In those troubled days, the Farmers Congress of Russia also gathered for an extraordinary meeting and decided that they would block delivery of agricultural products to the capital, if Yeltsin did not cancel the decree 1400.[20, 22]

A number of regions recognized Rutskoi as the legitimate acting president. The September 30 Meeting of the leaders of all republics, regions, and territories of the Russian Federation in the hall of the Constitutional Court adopted the anti-Yeltsin decisions.[20] Revolt of the province of the Russian Federation staggered the position of the president. Yeltsin understood that if he did not suppress resistance of the parliament by force immediately, later on he would have to fight with the province.

Supporters of the parliament in Moscow began organizing street protests. On September 28, 1993, a group of up to a thousand people tried to break through the cordon around the parliament, but they were dispersed by the policemen and troops of the Interior Ministry.

Meanwhile, news agencies demonstrated more and more shots of protesters beaten by the police; journalists themselves were battered by the riot police; mass media (domestic and foreign) exuded dissatisfaction with the actions of the executive power in Moscow. On top of that, Yeltsin team set rigid ideological control over the radio and TV, as in the old days of the communist party ruling.

Picture 3. Scuffles between the police and protesters (by unknown author, from http://psi-overlord.livejournal.com/1271522.html)

On September 29, after the public statement made by the U.S. Secretary of State Warren Christopher that the U.S. administration demanded from Yeltsin to ensure human rights in Moscow, including the rights of those who were in the parliament building, the situation became critical. A few hours after the US Secretary of State's speech, the White House released even a harsher statement demanding to cease use of force. Yeltsin understood the warning like that: he should not be the first to open fire; however, it was not possible to clear off the parliament building without the use of force. The executive power started readying for the decisive actions: on September 30, 1993, the newspaper Pravda reported "hasty preparations" in prisons: some inmates were being transferred in order to free more cells. The Minister of the Press and Information convened a meeting with chief editors of the pro-Yeltsin mass media and advised them to perceive "wisely and calmly" what was going to happen on October 4, 1993.[23]

The parliament was also well aware that they should not resort to the force, and they tried to avoid shooting at all cost; they feared provocations.

On Sunday of October 3 about three thousand of Muscovites - the crowd included women with children and elderly - held rallies in defense of the parliament and suspiciously easily captured the riot police's trucks and buses. They came to the parliament building, which had been unblocked by the time of the arrival of the crowd. Soon people at the parliament heard shots at the nearby Moscow Mayor's Office (the City Hall), which was guarded by the soldiers of the Interior Ministry.

Picture 4. Protesters at the parliament (by unknown author, from http://psi-overlord.livejournal.com/1271522.html)

The Commission of the State Duma, which investigated the October 1993 clash five years later, established that the shots were fired at the peaceful demonstration and at the windows of the parliament building.[24] The protesters rushed back, two people were wounded. Angered at the firing and encouraged by support of thousands people, acting President Rutskoi from a balcony of the parliament building called on the people to storm the City Hall.[25] It happened around 15:35 p.m. on October 3, 1993.

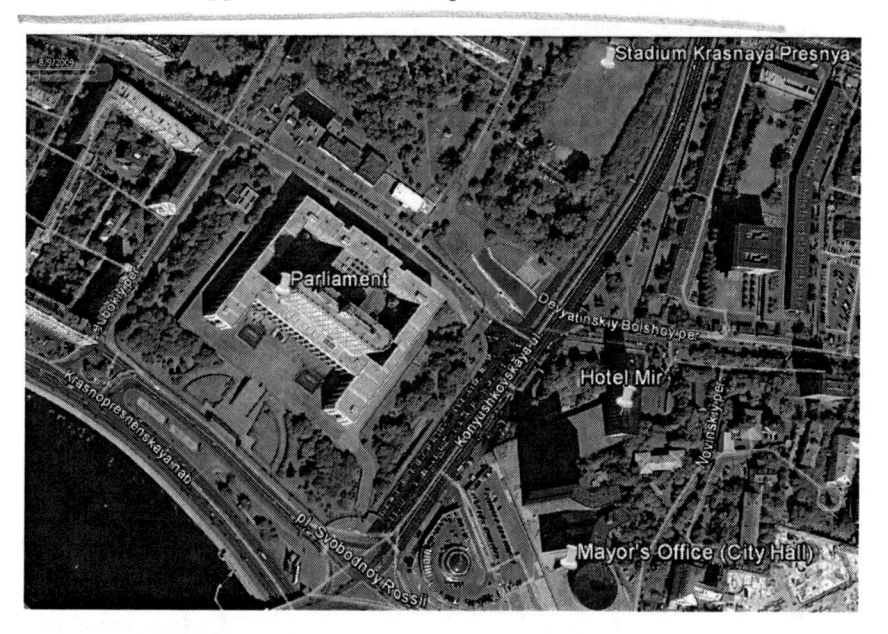

Picture 5. The Parliament building and the Moscow Mayor's Office (City Hall)

Meanwhile, at 16:00 p.m. Yeltsin signed a decree imposing the state of emergency in Moscow and suspending activities of all the opposition groups.

General Albert Makashov, following the Acting President Rutskoi's order, led the crowd to storm the City Hall. Having assessed the situation, Makashov got inside the building and via a megaphone advised the police to lay down their arms and surrender, guaranteeing their lives. The troopers of the Interior Ministry were kicked out of the building; there were about 200 of them, as Andrei Dunaev, Minister of the Interior appointed by the parliament, recalled in his interview to the Komsomolskaya Pravda at the 20th anniversary of the events. Dunaev also remembered that three of the soldiers of the Interior Ministry were killed by snipers from the roofs.

According to another version of the same events, an unknown man from the crowd fired at the troopers, killing one officer and wounding a few others. Much later, the prosecution will establish that some snipers fired from the roof of the Hotel Mir, which was next to the City Hall. These first casualties certainly looked like a provocation; the instigators were pushing the opposite sides to the use of arms and bloodshed.[25]

More than a dozen of military trucks and buses, abandoned by the units of the Interior Ministry, and the APCs that were previously used for cordoning off the building were seized by the crowd of pro-parliament protesters.[21] The APCs crews were let go, Dunaev recalled.

The jubilant parliament defenders inflated themselves to new achievements. Acting President Rutskoi ordered to capture the Ostankino TV Centre. General Makashov's group "North" consisting of 20 fighters loaded the military trucks and buses along with volunteers and set off to Ostankino;

Picture 6. The defenders of the Parliament (by unknown author, from http://psi-overlord.livejournal.com/1271522.html)

the Makashov's fighters were armed with assault rifles.[26] Eduard Limonov, a known writer and publicist, was in one of the buses. He recalled in his interview with journalist Victor Baranets of the Komsomolskaya Pravda on October 4, 2013 that they rode to Ostankino unarmed, joyfully shouting, "Hail to the Soviet Union!"

The rest of the protesters - the unarmed people - went off to Ostankino on foot. Eyewitness Lyudmila Surova recalled what the crowd that headed to Ostankino afoot looked like, "No fury, no animal fanaticism. Those were ordinary, but diverse people, my fellow citizens, my fellow countrymen. There were the young, the elderly, women, girls... Dad with his 10 year old son... We saw unorganized people... some intelligent and couth, others more aggressive... But they went not to kill, not to take revenge... What weapons did they carry? - Five or six metallic shields, one baton, a piece of a tap pipe, and a hatchet in the hands of a boy about 15 years old... There were no armed combat units." To stop an unarmed crowd like that was a piece of cake for the police. But nobody even tried; these people were trapped at the TV centre and shot. Surova titled her testimony *Report from the Site of Execution* and published it in the newspaper Nezavisimaya Gazeta on October 16, 1993 (the excerpt is taken from the book *The Great Russian Tragedy* by Ruslan Khasbulatov).[20]

What happened at the Ostankino TV Centre is known from testimonies of a number of eye witnesses and investigations of historians.[27, 28, 29]

On October 3, 1993, the Ostankino TV Centre was guarded by 87 officers of the Moscow Office of the Interior and by 20 military personnel. They were armed with 85 handguns and 56 assault rifles. By 4:30 p.m. 84 more soldiers arrived to the TV centre; they did not have firearms but were equipped with body armor, helmets and rubber truncheons. By 5 p.m. arrived six armored personnel carriers with 105 officers of the Interior Ministry's special forces (the Vityaz group) and 14 soldiers armed with machine guns. The Vityaz took up positions at the doors of the 17th porch and erected barriers blocking the entrance. By 7 p.m. 155 more pro-Yeltsin military and police arrived with handguns and assault rifles. In total they were armed with not less than 320 assault and sniper rifles and machine guns, 130 handguns, 12 grenade launchers including antitank grenade launcher RPG-7 and sufficient amount of ammunition. Pro-presidential military concentrated quite a formidable force at the TV centre to confront the protesters.

The group "North" led by General Makashov had reached the television center by about 5 p.m. At some point, the Makashov fighters were joined by young people carrying an antitank grenade launcher RPG-7 (taken away from the riot police) and two grenades to it. Upon arrival on trucks, the pro-parliament fighters came to the 17th porch, where they held a spontaneous meeting. Makashov called on the protesters to keep order, asking not to break anything in the television center because it was the state property.

Picture 7. The Ostankino TV Centre

The pro-Yeltsin officers in charge went out of the television centre for negotiations. General Makashov with some of his people climbed up the porch to them. Makashov demanded to surrender the television center, provide a TV operator, and give an opportunity to the leaders of the Supreme Soviet to go live. The police officers replied that they could not surrender without an order. Makashov, having agreed with their arguments, gave them time to connect with their superiors. Thus, the police officers bought time for their reinforcements to come. Finally, they informed Makashov that they had received a positive answer, but the video translation would have to be done from another building, and they advised him to go there. Believing the promises, Makashov with his people moved to the technical centre. Most of the other protesters, who arrived with Makashov on trucks and buses, moved to the technical centre, too.

Makashov advised the pro-Yeltsin people and, in particular, the special forces that the unarmed, peaceful pro-parliament demonstration was about to approach the television centre and asked not to fire at them accidentally. Makashov guaranteed to the commander of Vityaz that the demonstrators would not make any shots.

After the fruitless waiting, General Makashov put forward an ultimatum demanding from the police to lay down their firearms and unlock the entrance door. The police officer carrying out the negotiations refused to surrender. Makashov warned that in three minutes he would start the assault. Two his trucks rammed the glass door to the technical center and a window next to it, and the unarmed general went to the lobby to talk to the police officers. He sternly warned the special forces against starting any shooting and gave them time to leave the building. It was a few minutes after 7 p.m.

Picture 8. The truck is breaking the glass entrance to the Ostankino technical centre (by unknown author, from http://psi-overlord.livejournal.com/1271522.html)

In the next few minutes a massive bloodshed started. Historians still do not know who triggered it, despite the crowd of witnesses (though most of them were shot on the spot). It is known that the first shot was made from the roof of the television center by a trooper of the special forces Vityaz. The fire came without any warning. Apparently, the sniper aimed to put down a man with a grenade launcher - a student who was figuring out how to mount a grenade;[28] the sniper wounded a man right next to the student.[27] Not many people in the crowd at the TV centre noticed the first shot and the wounded man. It would be fair to say that the first sniper's shot did not play any significant role in provoking the rage. It was the following shot, more accurately, a fatal blast, that triggered the bloodshed.

In his book *Anafema*, eye witness Ivan Ivanov recalled that right after the first sniper's shot "an officer [from the Makashov group] approached the general and said to him that a cap had not been removed off the RPG - it wouldn't fire. Makashov replied that no one was going to shoot anyway." And literally four minutes after that talk Ivanov heard popping of two or three grenades at once; they were fired from the TV centre.[28] The grenades blew up at the feet of the student with the RPG and people next to him.

Officers guarding the technical centre also heard an explosion inside, as a result of which one of the Vityaz commandos (Nikolai Sitnikov) was killed. Around 7:30 p.m., a few moments after the explosions inside and outside the technical center, the pro-Yeltsin forces opened a heavy gunfire at the people that stood near the entrance. All of them were killed except for one man. Within an hour, more than half of the Makashov fighters were shot. Captain Eugene Shtukaturov, the head of the Makashov security, brought the survivors out of the gunfire to the Ostankino tower square where they hid behind the trees. He was arrested along with Makashov the next day.

Until 1998, it was generally believed that the first blast was made from the Makashov's grenade launcher RPG-7, probably by Shtukaturov.[27] Yeltsin wrote in his book *Notes of the President* that it was that fatal grenade shot that forced the Vityaz commandos to open the gunfire.[30] It was the very same opportunity the pro-Yeltsin side had been waiting for in order to "legitimately" use force against the parliament.

In 1998, Leonid Proshkin, one of the prosecutors who investigated the riots in Moscow in October of 1993 (it was the classified criminal case 18/123669-93), disclosed to the newspaper Sovershenno Sekretno that soldier Sitnikov was not killed by the Makashov's RPG-7. The place of the incident was examined by the leading expert on grenade launchers of the Missile and Artillery Directorate of the General Staff of the Russian Armed Forces, and he concluded that there was no RPG-7 grenade explosion in the room where Sitnikov died. Thus, the prosecution refuted the version of the pro-Yeltsin commandos who claimed that they opened the fire in response to the blast that had killed their teammate Sitnikov.[29] Likely, Sitnikov was killed by a shot that came from inside the technical centre, or some of his firearms accidentally exploded.

Eduard Limonov, who was among the protesters at the technical centre, recalled that they experienced surreal feelings at the moment: a crazy guy rode his bicycle under the bullets and through the flames (a nearby fuel truck took fire), an accordionist played a waltz, and some old men bravely run around under the heavy gunfire.

Meanwhile the unarmed protesters, who set off to Ostankino on foot, finally reached the TV centre and were met with the machine-gun fire. Six delegates from the protesters - employees of the Interior Ministry who sided with the parliament - came out to explain to the Vityaz commandos that the demonstrators were unarmed and asked for a ceasefire. The special forces ceased fire for half an hour and requested all the protesters step outside the fenced territory of the TV center. Once the people got behind the fence, the Vityaz methodically shot them with automatic guns and sniper rifles.[27,28,29]

The pro-Yeltsin forces fired at everyone, without distinction by age or sex; they shot people who tried to hide or run, the ones who lay on the ground and the ones who assisted the wounded, people in white medical coats and journalists. Among them there were two friends: Americans Terry Michael Duncan, a lawyer, and Otto Pohl, a freelance photographer for The New York Times.

Otto and Terry repeatedly asked the Vityaz commandos not to fire at them and give them an opportunity to get out of the fire zone, because they were foreign journalists. The soldiers just swore and intensified shooting. Finally, one officer from the special forces allowed them to leave. Otto rose from the flower bed and immediately was hit by shrapnel in the chest from the Ostankino technical centre. The Vityaz commandos did not let anybody crawl to Pohl to stanch his bleeding; they shot the ones who tried to approach the wounded man. Duncan, while in the vicinity, talked and cheered Pohl so that his friend would not lose consciousness. This went on for some time, until Duncan was wounded, too. When Pohl looked over, he noticed that Duncan's head was bloody. Finally, several men pulled Pohl out of the gunfire. The photographer advised them that there was another wounded American. One of the protesters (his last name was Mikhailov, as the prosecution established later) attempted to persuade the soldiers to let him take wounded Duncan away. Mikhailov, waving his hand, got up and walked to Duncan but did not reach him because he was killed by a machine gun shot in the back. Other men pulled Duncan by his leg out of the fire zone and carried away.[27, 29, 30, 31] Northern-Irish freelance cameraman Rory Peck was also killed by Yeltsin's loyalists while he was covering the events at the Ostankino centre. Peck was posthumously awarded the Order for Personal Courage by Yeltsin.[32]

The shooting lasted all night and next day, resulting in 46 people killed and 124 wounded.[—, 33]

Oleg Fochkin and Dmitri Bolgarov were the first journalists who managed to access the famous criminal case 18/123669-93, and some of the testimonies from that case are below.

N. Razov witnessed, "I remember well how a 'Ural' truck hit the glass door of the complex. No one came out of there. After a while, APCs [the pro-Yeltsin military] - the ones that followed us on the way to Ostankino - approached the building. At this point, people fell silent, waiting for further actions of the military. The APCs opened fire at the building. The protesters became jubilant. I remember shouts: 'Hurrah! The army is on our side!' and 'What are we waiting for? Let's storm! We will be supported!' Then the APCs drove closer and opened fire at the protesters. Clearly, they fired to kill."[34]

For a long time it was believed that the first APCs' shots at the technical centre were a tactical maneuver to gain confidence of the protesters and get closer to the pro-parliament crowd. Officer Alexandr M. was a member of the crew of one of those APCs. He explained what happened: "Our first shots at the building were a response to the fire from the technical centre. Later an order came to fire at the crowd."[34]

Security guard Andrei M. sat out most of the shooting under the table in the lobby. He said, "It was a very strange feeling. On one side there was mad drunken mob, on the other - totally insane Vityaz commandos (enlisted 18-year-old boys). They reached for weapons at every suspicious sound. There was no coherence in their actions. Everything was happening very quickly, but I do remember that the first shots were fired from the back, from the Vityaz group. To be more precise, these were not shots, but blasts."[34]

Later, Defense Minister Pavel Grachev admitted that the Ostankino TV Centre was defended by 400 military personnel and the infamous Vityaz, and six APCs; they were later reinforced by additional 450 servicemen of the Interior Ministry with arms and necessary ammunition. The military personnel and the special forces were well equipped (helmets, body armor, sniper guns, machine guns, communication devices, night vision devices); the pro-parliament Makashov fighters and peaceful protesters had little to no protection at all. The pro-Yeltsin forces were professionals, specially trained for combat fighting. The pro-parliament crowd, according to the information of the Interior Ministry, consisted of about four thousand unarmed and a hundred armed people. As for the weapons, the attackers had one grenade launcher (which probably did not fire), and 20 to 80 (according to various sources) machine guns.[20, 23]

What happened in Ostankino should be called a massacre. And responsibility for the mass killing of the opposition lies on General Pavel Golubets, Deputy Commander of the Interior Ministry's troops, and Sergei Lysyuk, Commander of the 6th Special Forces Detachment Vityaz. Having absolute superiority over the people who came to Ostankino, among which there were only twenty professional fighters (the Makashov group), they acted disproportionately and indiscriminately.[27] Later, the Vityaz was praised and rewarded by Yeltsin.

At the time the news painted a different picture for the general public, especially in the province: the pro-Yeltsin forces defended the TV centre from "mortal" danger, from "dire" threats of the "red-brown rebels" who wanted to go live on the air. As if it would have changed anything, if Makashov had been aired. Not to mention that the Ostankino TV Centre could have been cut off of power, as was previously done to the parliament building. Clearly, had the pro-Yeltsin forces intended just to limit the parliament's access to the TV channels, it could have been done much easier and with no casualties at all.

Picture 9. Victims of the civil war of 1993 (by unknown author, from http://psi-overlord.livejournal.com/1271522.html)

Obviously, they needed to inflate hysteria and fear of the "red-brown terror". If the events of those days had been fully covered by the news agencies, it would have become apparent that the "assault" of the TV centre was just shooting of mostly unarmed opposition. And the pro-Yeltsin forces would not have looked "heroes". It had been enough to let the general public see how the protesters, including curious onlookers like Terry Duncan, were being mercilessly shot, illuminated by the APCs' headlights for better view, the whole country would have decisively sided with the parliament.

Yeltsin's speech *To the Citizens of Russia* on the night of October 3-4, 1993 abounded words "bandits" and "thugs", "gangs of mercenary troops accustomed to killing and tyranny", "killed unarmed Muscovites", "raised their hands against civilians, against Moscow, against Russia, children, women and old people", "we'll protect our children, our mothers and fathers", "we'll stop and disarm thugs and assassins". We, in the province, were puzzled hearing the Yeltsin's message. Majority of the protesters were older people - our mothers and fathers - that sided with the parliament protesting against the Gaidar's shock therapy. Though they were called "bandits", none of the people killed had criminal records, as the prosecution established later. The only group that could be branded as "red-brown" among defenders of the parliament was the Barkashov nationalists (about a hundred people); but they did not play a significant role in the uprising. Nevertheless, they were used by Yeltsin's propaganda to justify the massacre at the Ostankino centre and the subsequent shelling of the parliament.

It's worth noting that Gennady Zyuganov, the leader of the "red" Communist Party of the Russian Federation, was not present among the protesters or defenders of the parliament during October 3-4 events. While the majority of the parliament opposition was denied access to the TV channels, Zyuganov was invited by the pro-Yeltsin forces to speak out on the TV. He played a role of the "wise peacemaker" between both sides. Thus he saved his party from dissolution; later he was allowed to participate in the State Duma (a new parliament) elections. The shooting of the parliament swept from the political arena almost all Zyuganov's competitors from the left camp.

The cruelty of the reprisal at Ostankino surprised even those who sided with Yeltsin. Mikhail Leontiev, a journalist that hated the parliament, said to the pro-Yeltsin newspaper Segodnya, "We are told and showed how the gangs of brutal nationalist-communist thugs roamed around Moscow, storming the television center, the City Hall, and various other socially desired objects. However, you will not find any reports of smashed defenseless commercial booths. Horrible communist expropriators, having rested under the heavy gunfire at Ostankino, ran off to a nearby kiosk to **buy for money** vodka and chocolates and returned to die for the ideals of the social justice. The kiosks at the parliament building had made record revenues over the "night of lawlessness", when the cordons were removed, when one could not find a single policeman in the city [the night of

October 3-4, 1993]."[23]

After the shooting at Ostankino the pro-Yeltsin Security Council convened a meeting. The main problem was to convince Defense Minister Pavel Grachev to use the army for shelling of the parliament without a written order from Yeltsin. Ivan Ivanov witnessed what was happening at the meeting and described it in his book *Anafema: Chronicles of the Coup D'état*: a captain from the presidential security suggested that the special forces storm two porches (24th and the one that led to the Khasbulatov's apartments) and kill Khasbulatov and Rutskoi, or start a tank or helicopter shelling of the parliament at dawn. Yeltsin liked the idea with the tanks.[28]

Closer to 3.00 a.m., when the Defense Minister Grachev finally agreed to use the army against the opposition, senior military officers were invited one by one to his office at the Security Council. The commander of the 119th Naro-Fominsk parachute regiment was called first. The task to the regiment was set apart from all others, but his vainglorious commander, coming out of door after receiving the order, quickly disclosed to everybody, "We are to block all approaches to the building!"[28]

At the time, the 119th parachute regiment was scheduled to move from Kaunas (its previous location) to some distant region. At the last moment Minister Grachev had changed the plan and moved them to Naro-Fominsk near Moscow, where they were unwelcomed guests and did not expect to receive living quarters any time soon. For the successful execution of the people's deputies on October 4, 1993, the entire regiment was rewarded with housing. Apparently, that was the condition on which they agreed to participate.[28] The defenders of the parliament had expected that the 119th Naro-Fominsk regiment would side with them - after all, Vice President Rutskoi was one of their kinds, a colonel of an air assault regiment; but the opposition hoped in vain. The 119th regiment, as well as the special forces Vityaz, covered itself with shame that will not be forgotten any time soon.

Next was called the commander of the legendary Taman Division and was given a task to bring his tanks to the parliament building. Minister Grachev expressed confidence that a couple of shots by the tanks would be enough to make the people's deputies and their supporters come out and give up resistance, but many officers gloomily chuckled at that. According to the plan of the operation, a squadron of tanks would make "only" one shot each, and either the frightened parliament would surrender or the special forces would begin the assault.[28]

The special forces Alpha (the counter-terrorism group "A" of the former KGB), Vympel (the diversionary - special operations - unit of the former 1st KGB Directorate) received a task to ensure the passage to the building and take the first floor by storm. When the commanders of the Alpha and the Vympel were asked, "Will you carry out the order of the President?" they replied, "We were not trained in shooting at unarmed typists."[28]

About 4 a.m., in the Kremlin, Yeltsin finally signed a written order to use the military, as the president admitted in his book.[30] By the Defense Minister Grachev's directive, tanks of the Taman Division arrived in Moscow, and he personally led a column of the 119th parachute regiment and personally gave the order: "Follow me! In case of any firing at the column, shoot to kill!" There are video materials documenting as Grachev took the binoculars off his eyes and with a satisfied smile ordered the tank crews, "Come on, piss them off!"[28]

Picture 10. Tanks of the Taman Division are shelling at the parliament (from http://ros1993.narod.ru/93_10_04.htm)

The mass media reported that on the same night Gaidar, the former prime minister of Yeltsin's government, was trying to get 11 billion rubles cash from the Central Bank to pay for the execution of the parliament. He sent Deputy Finance Minister Vavilov for the money that night, but the Central Bank refused to give such an astronomical sum of cash; then Vavilov went straight to GosZnak (the state institution that printed the banknotes) and simply confiscated one billion rubles. This was the first portion of boons for the shooting teams. The second one - 11 billion rubles - Gaidar obtained from the Central Bank a few days later. This money ensured Yeltsin's victory. Several army officers and two divisional commanders agreed for the generous fee to cover the Russian army with shame and blood of their fellow citizens.[28]

In the morning of October 4, 1993 armed clashes took place between the Defense Ministry's Taman Division and 119th parachute regiment on one side, and the Interior Ministry's Division of APCs on the other side; all of them belonged to pro-Yeltsin forces. This story defies imagination of even the most experienced, seasoned officers: for several hours at the heart of Moscow the defense minister and the interior minister could not coordinate the actions of their subordinates!

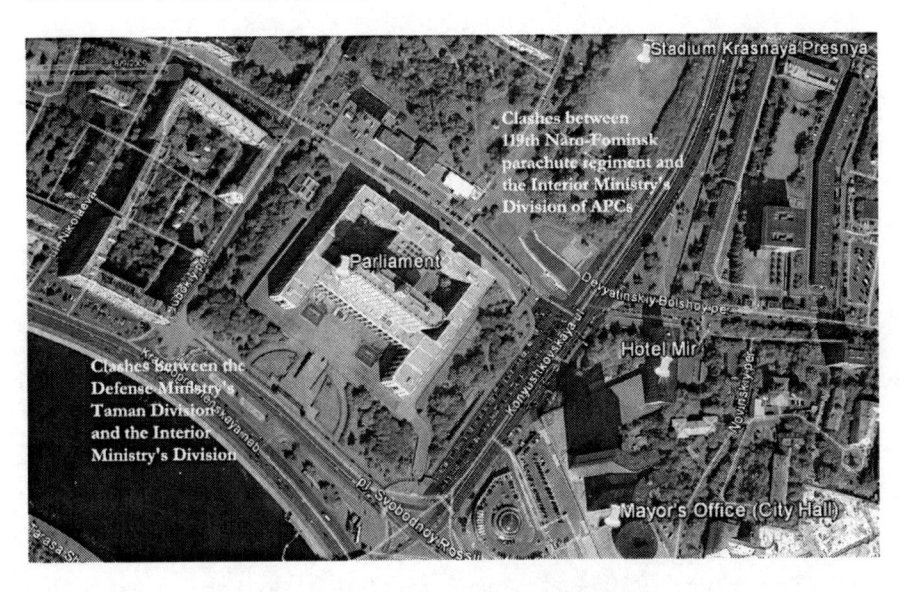

Picture 11. Armed clashes between pro-Yeltsin's forces

As a result of the longer than three-hour fight, several APCs were knocked out and ten people killed. Ministers, as well as the killed officers and soldiers, were awarded with the highest government decorations. The October 4 shooting between the defense ministry's and the interior ministry's units was a closely guarded secret for some time. The officers who participated in the shootings explained to the prosecution that they did not know who fought against them. They were ordered to fire at everybody who had weapons.[29]

Historian Valery Shevchenko in his work *Forgotten Victims of October 1993* argued that in the early morning hours of October 4, 1993, there were about 5,000 people inside the parliament building and 1,000 - 1,500 on the nearby streets.[35] And around 6:50 a.m. their mass murdering began.[20, 21, 28]

The assault and execution of the parliament started suddenly, without any announcement or warning. The pro-Yeltsin attackers had neither offered to surrender, nor let women and children (yes, there were children inside!) leave the building. The first shots from the APCs killed about forty unarmed people. Rutskoi repeatedly demanded to cease fire and allow women and children leave, but it had no effect on the military - the fire did not stop for 10 hours!

7:25 a.m. Five infantry fighting vehicles (BMPs) moved through the barricades to the square in front of the parliament building.

8 a.m. BMPs and ACPs fired at the parliament windows.

9 a.m. The defenders of the parliament shot at the advancing military units. The pro-Yeltsin armored vehicles fired from heavy machine guns and cannons at the 12th and 13th floors, setting them on fire. People inside the parliament were demoralized; the opposition fought back sluggishly: the Alpha fighters noted that the parliament defenders did not use their anti-tank grenade launchers. Veronica Kutsyllo, a journalist of the newspaper Kommersant, who was in the building during the entire assault, had not seen anybody shooting out of the windows at the besiegers.

9:20 a.m. Tanks from the Kalinin (Novoarbatsky) bridge began shelling of the upper floors of the parliament. Six T-80 tanks participated in the bombardment and fired supposedly 12 shells.[21]

11:25 a.m. Intensive artillery fire resumed. By this hour, hospitals had already assisted 192 victims, 158 people were hospitalized, 18 - died, according to the Chief Medical Office in Moscow.[21]

3 p.m. Snipers from the roofs of high-rises adjacent to the parliament building opened fire at the police and the nearby bystanders. Who were these snipers? Which side did they take? It remains unknown. Two soldiers were wounded and two journalists and one woman were killed by them.

The special forces Alpha and Vympel drove up to the building to take the parliament by storm. They saw dead and wounded people on the ground and tried to evacuate them. And then the bullet of an unknown sniper fatally shot Gennady Sergeyev, Lieutenant of the Alpha. Some of the Sergeyev people told journalists later that the bullet that killed his commander did not come from the parliament building. Someone purposely fired at them to provoke their rage, and the Alpha professionals immediately realized that.

At about 4 p.m., Colonel Sergey Protsenko, the head of the Vympel unit, entered the parliament building practically unarmed and let the defenders know that the special forces were ordered to take the parliament by storm. Both the Alpha and the Vympel had legendary reputations; the parliament defenders would not stand a chance against them. Colonel Protsenko successfully negotiated with Alexandr Rutskoi a voluntary surrender and suggested everyone to leave the building under the Alpha escort, promising safety on the streets and passage to the subway. He managed to persuade them to surrender by 5 p.m. To continue resistance was futile. The besiegers' next stage of the assault included use of gas and gunships. Yeltsin was playing for broke.

The commanders of both groups of the special forces complied with the presidential order, but did it in their own way - it was their initiative to persuade the leadership of the parliament to a peaceful surrender; it was them who secured evacuation of part of the people from the burning parliament. Nobody had instructed them to negotiate with the people's deputies. Without firing a shot, the Alpha and Vympel commandos brought out of the building about 100 people through a live corridor they formed to protect the surrendered.

The Alpha's and Vympel's officers managed to put down a few snipers that were trying to kill more of the commandos to incite hatred against the parliament. In addition, Vympel knocked out a maddened crew of one of the APCs, which fired from the heavy machine gun at both the pro-Yeltsin and the pro-parliament people.

According to eyewitnesses, the Alpha and Vympel commandos behaved very decently in this difficult situation. They treated people quite differently than the riot police; the work of the latter was accompanied by atrocities. The riot policemen yelled at the parliament defenders coming out of the building and beat them with rifle butts, treating people like they were bandits. In comparison, the Alpha officers were saying, "Drop your hands. You are not prisoners of war." The commandos' live corridor prevented attacks of drunken youths that enjoyed watching the execution of the parliament.

The Alpha and Vympel commandos (in particular, Sergei Klimeniev) informed reporters that it was hardly accidental that the provocateurs and hooligans fired at the officers of the special forces and at the crowd of onlookers from nearby rooftops. Officer V. Shurygin saw snipers who shot at the police. Unknown snipers also fired at the soldiers of the Sofrinsky Brigade, which sided with the parliament. Obviously, the snipers' job was to inflate rage on both sides.[22]

A bit of light was shed on the snipers' mystery by journalists. According to the publication in the Novaya Ezhednevnaya Gazeta on October 20, 1993, some of the snipers were employees of the Interior Ministry.[23]

The Alpha officers let journalists of the newspaper Izvestia know that their superiors wanted them to shed more blood and kill the "rebel" leaders during the assault.[22] The Alpha did not "understand" this order, and "somebody above" became very unhappy with them. Most of the Alpha commandos were struck off of the honor list. Later the pro-Yeltsin government disbanded the elite KGB unit Vympel and resubdued its remains to the Interior Ministry; most of its officers retired.

The history of the withdrawal of the elite special forces of the KGB from participation in the shooting of the parliament deserves a separate discussion. All of the combat professionals either practically disobeyed the

Kremlin as the Alpha and the Vympel, or openly "sent" Yeltsin far away, like Colonel Vasiliev, the commander of the Sofrinsky Brigade of the special operations. The only exception was Sergei Lysyuk, the commander of the division Vityaz of the special forces of the Interior Ministry, who covered himself and his subordinates with shame at Ostankino on October 3, 1993.

Massive surrender of the parliament defenders began after 5 p.m. About 700 people holding hands behind their heads left the building walking between two rows of the riot police. Those who were coming out in the direction of the City Hall were mercilessly beaten and forwarded to a "filtration camp" in one of the neighboring basements.

At 5:30 p.m., Alexandr Rutskoi, Albert Makashov, and Ruslan Khasbulatov demanded that the ambassadors of the western countries provided them with a guarantee of their safety; around 6 p.m. they were arrested and under escort of paratroopers and officers from the Yeltsin security were delivered by bus to the detention center in Lefortovo. According to Alexandr Korzhakov, the head of the Yeltsin security, who was in charge of their arrest, he had a task of killing Rutskoi and Khasbulatov: "But it was not possible, because they hid in the crowd of deputies."[36]

The pro-Yeltsin forces went wild. They tried to kill even the president of Kalmykia, Kirsan Ilyumzhinov, who negotiated the terms of surrender with Rutskoi. Ilyumzhinov managed to hide in his seven-ton vehicle that rammed through the barricades to get away from the pursuers. The riot policemen intercepted Ilyumzhinov's security guards and heavily beat them with rifle butts.

In the nearby yards the riot police raged even fiercer. They arranged a gangster-like "pipeline" there. They beat people with boots and rifle butts in the kidney and groin areas; they beat everybody. They staged mock executions for the people's deputies: put them with their faces to the wall and fired over their heads from the machine guns. If captured people wore military uniform, they were isolated and killed.

In the police stations, arrested people - the parliament supporters, as well as just simple onlookers - were forced to give false testimonies as if they had seen heavily armed people's deputies (majority of the people's deputies did not know how to hold a gun - they were just ordinary civilians). The detainees who resisted were mercilessly beaten. The detention centers were overcrowded. The savage torturing of people continued over the night.[37]

The mass violence was accompanied by looting. Commercial booths near the parliament, as well as trailers with food, were smashed and robbed. The riot policemen turned inside out everybody's pockets confiscating money and personal belonging, stripping people off of jackets and caps. The parliament building was plundered, too; a crowd of looters was stealing computers, telephones, paintings, and even the contents of cupboards.

Picture 12. Traces of shooting in the centre of Moscow (by unknown author, from http://psi-overlord.livejournal.com/1271522.html)

Below is the excerpt from the report of the Commission on Human Rights published by the Nezavisimaya Gazeta on July 23, 1994: "According to the Prosecutor General's Office, more than 6,000 people were kept in Moscow's temporary detention isolators between October 3 and 5; half of them without registration ... of their detention."[37] The detainees were heavily beaten. Witnesses testified that especially brutal drubbing took place at the 18th, 48th, 77th, 100th and 119th police stations. The Moscow's Prosecutor's Office received 115 complaints from citizens, mainly related to the beating by the law enforcement officers. But majority of the victims did not complain of the executions, fearing deployment of political repressions. From September 21 to October 5, 1993, seventy two journalists were injured in Moscow, seven of them died. Six journalists suffered from the supporters of the parliament, and the other sixty six - from the pro-Yeltsin police and military.[37]

Historian Valery Shevchenko provided recollections of dozens of witnesses in his book *The Forgotten Victims of October 1993*.[35] Some of them are below.

People's deputy A. Leontiev recalled, "Six APCs stood on the street in front of the parliament, and the Kuban Cossacks lay between them and the building, behind the barbed wire - about a hundred of people. They were unarmed; they just wore the Cossack uniform... No more than 5-6 of them reached the porches of the parliament; the rest were killed."

After the assault, the President of Kalmykia Kirsan Ilyumzhinov said in one of his interviews, "I saw that in the building there were not 50 or 70 dead bodies, but hundreds. At first, the alive tried to gather the corpses in one place, but then they abandoned the idea: it was dangerous to make a move. Most of the victims were unarmed, incidental people. By the time we got there, more than 500 were dead. By the end of the day, I think, that figure had grown to thousands."

On the evening of October 4, 1993, the President of Ingushetia Ruslan Aushev told Stanislav Govoruhin, a movie producer and a politician, that he eye witnessed how 127 corpses were carried out of the parliament building, but a lot was still inside.

The tank shelling significantly increased the death toll, though the military claimed that they fired harmless blank shells. Defense Minister Pavel Grachev said, "We shot six blanks from one tank at one pre-selected window to force the conspirators to leave the parliament building. We knew that the office with that window was empty," (cited from the book by historian Valery Shevchenko).[35] However, some witnesses - journalists of the newspaper Moskovskie Novosti, who watched the tank firing at the parliament, argued that the Grachev's shells did not look like blanks: they punched through the building, each projectile breaking 5-10 windows, causing fires, and making thousands of paper sheets flew out of the opposite side of the building.[35]

I found many more heartrending testimonies in the Shevchenko's book:[35]

I. Savelyeva, who went out of the parliament towards the embankment, recalled that the police pushed her in the direction of the residential buildings on Glubokiy Pereulok, where the riot police behaved especially ferociously: "The porch, where we were pushed to, was full of people. Shouts were heard from the upper floors. Everyone was searched, ripped off of jackets and coats. They looked for the military personnel and the police officers who sided with the parliament, and as soon as they were identified, they were immediately taken away somewhere..." Yuri Vlasov, an Olympic champion, testified that everyone who was in the first porch was killed after being tortured; women were stripped naked, gang raped, and then shot. People's deputy V. Kotelnikov remembered: "We ran into the courtyard, a huge old square courtyard. In our group there were about 15 people... When we reached the last porch, there remained only three of us... We climbed up to the attic - the doors were broken, luckily for us. We hid among the rubbish behind a sort of pipe and stopped moving... We decided to lie low. It was curfew, the place was cordoned off by the riot police, and we were practically in their camp. The shots continued throughout all night. When the dawn broke ... we slowly descended. When I opened the door, I almost fainted. The whole courtyard was littered with corpses, in a checkerboard-like pattern. All the corpses were in unusual positions: some sat, some lay on the side, some with a raised leg, some with a raised hand, and all of them were bluish-yellow. I wondered what was unusual in that picture. And then I figured: they all were naked, all naked..."

Those who went out of the building in the direction of the stadium Krasnaya Presnya also had tragic fate. Executions at the stadium began in the early evening on October 4. According to the residents of the adjoining apartment buildings who saw how the arrested were shot, "this bloody orgy lasted all night". The first group was driven to a concrete fence of the stadium by gunmen in a mottled camouflage. Then they fired with heavy machine gun at the people who stood at the stadium fence. Later, already in twilight, second group was shot."

Alexandr Lapin spent in the stadium's "death chamber" three days from evening of October 4 till October 7: "Once the parliament had fallen, its defenders were taken to the stadium wall. The riot police isolated those who were in the Cossack, police, or military uniform or just dressed in camouflage, or who had any party membership documents, from the ones like me who did not have anything of that sort. ... We saw our comrades being shot in the back... Then we were herded into a locker room... We were kept there for three days. Without food and water, and most importantly, without tobacco. Twenty of us..."

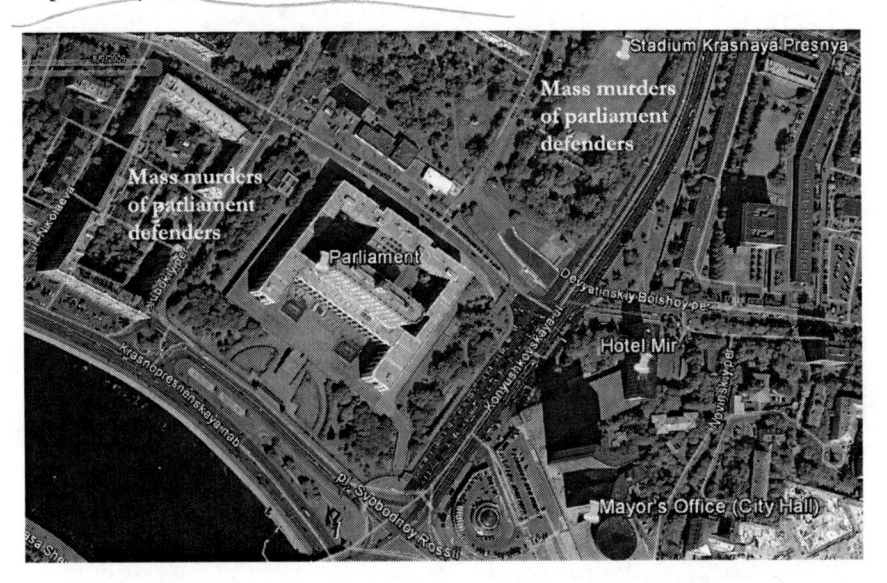

Picture 13. Places of execution of the defenders of the parliament

To be fair to the riot police, I need to admit that there were decent people among them, too. One group of the military officers, who defended the parliament, left the building through the underground communications and headed towards the subway, when they were spotted by the riot police. The policemen advised them to climb up and promised that they would let them go. The policemen did let them go even without checking the defenders' documents. Only one guy - a lieutenant colonel, the senior of the defenders' group - refused to climb up and shot himself. The commander of the riot police group worried that he would be blamed for the lt.-colonel's death, but one of the lt.-colonel's associates offered to confirm that their senior killed himself, and the corpse was registered as a suicide. This story was told to Victor Baranets, a journalist of the Komsomolskaya Pravda, and was published by him on the twentieth anniversary of the October 1993' events.

How many people were killed or injured on October 3-4, 1993? At the time, staff of the morgues and hospitals refused to answer questions about the number of victims, referring to the order from their headquarters. "For two days I had been telephoning dozens of Moscow hospitals and morgues, trying to find out the number of victims. I got replies that this was the classified information," journalist Yuri Igonin said in his article in the newspaper Retch in November of 1993.[38]

A large number of corpses soon disappeared from the Moscow morgues. Physician of the Rescue Center of the Moscow Medical Academy A. Dalnov, who worked in the parliament building during the assault, said a few days after the shooting, "They are doing cleanup, and the exact number of victims will never be known. All materials in the Centre for Emergency Medicine related to September 21 - October 4, 1993 are classified. Some case histories of wounded and dead have been re-written; dates of their admittance to morgues and hospitals have been changed. Part of the victims, in accordance with the State Medical Directorate instructions, has been transported to the morgues of nearby towns." Dalnov believed that the death toll was underestimated by at least one order of magnitude. Dalnov and his colleagues also visited hospitals and morgues of the Ministries of Defense, Interior and State Security. They learned that the bodies of victims of the October tragedy, who were kept there, were not included in the official reports.[35]

Prosecutor General Valentin Stepankov claimed that they did not find any dead bodies - not even one - in the parliament building when they visited it on October 5, 1993. Therefore, the prosecution could not fully establish the cause of deaths of the victims.

The Commission of the State Duma, which investigated the October 1993 events in 1998-1999, concluded that about 200 people were killed or died of wounds and not less than 1,000 people were injured in the clash of September 21 - October 5, 1993.[24]

Our hearts ache when I think of the atrocities committed by my own kin to others of my kin. The Supreme Soviet and the Congress of the People's Deputies were the legitimate sovereign power in the country. Why did Yeltsin punish so severely the defenders of the parliament, throwing at the deputies and their mostly unarmed defenders 3,000 soldiers and officers, 10 tanks, 80 ACPs, 20 BMPs, 15 armored reconnaissance and patrol vehicles, over 60 light infantry fighting vehicles?[39, 40]

It was the Congress of People's Deputies that pulled Yeltsin out of political oblivion, appointing him the Chairman of the Supreme Soviet in 1990. It was the Supreme Soviet that convened a referendum to establish the post of the President of Russia. It was the Supreme Soviet that strongly supported Yeltsin in the first year of his presidency.

In August 1991, during the "putsch", the State Emergency Committee did not dare to send military to the parliament building to arrest Yeltsin and his associates fearing to shed blood of their own people. Yeltsin did not repeat this mistake in October 1993 and dauntlessly ordered to shoot civilians, stigmatizing defenders of the parliament as "bandits", "thugs", "gangs of assassins", and "red-brown terrorists".

The forensic ballistic examination carried out on fragments of the bullets recovered from the victims of October 1993 events proved that no one (the examined corpses) was killed by the firearms confiscated from the defenders of the Supreme Soviet.[41] The prosecution also intended to perform the same ballistic examination on the firearms of the pro-Yeltsin forces, but their request was denied.

Yeltsin was not happy with the results of the investigation, which revealed that soldier Sitnikov of the Vityaz was not killed by the Makashov's grenade at the Ostankino TV Centre. Soon the prosecutors were ordered to stop the investigation.[41]

Arrested defenders of the parliament, along with Rutskoi and Khasbulatov, were sent to the Lefortovo remand centre. Five months later, they were released without a trial. In the name of the new constitution and the national reconciliation, all participants of the events of October 1993, as well as of August 1991, were granted amnesty.

Captain Eugene Shtukaturov, who allegedly triggered the bloodshed at Ostankino, a decade later headed in Moscow the Interior Ministry's center of military-patriotic education for youth and became friends with some of the officers from the Vityaz who were his foes in 1993.[27] The two opposite sides in the Russian "small civil war" have reconciled with each other over the past years.

PARLIAMENT FELL VICTIM OF YELTSIN'S LUST FOR POWER

Yeltsin's propaganda claimed that the Supreme Soviet started an armed insurgency, and Yeltsin was forced to react accordingly. This is absolutely false.

Alexandr Tarasov, a prominent political analyst and a left-wing sociologist, performed a detailed analysis and unequivocally proved in his book *Provocation. A Version of Events in Moscow on October 3-4, 1993* that the parliament was taken unawares by the Yeltsin's decree and subsequent shooting. The parliament was not preparing any "mutiny" and absolutely was not ready for it, unlike the other side.[23]

Tarasov argued:

> The 'conspirators' did not prepare their associates from various organizations for such a turn of events - and that's why it came as a surprise to practically all potential defenders of the parliament.
>
> The 'conspirators' neither pulled to Moscow its combat-ready supporters from the province, nor spread them out in the city and the closest suburbs, nor armed them in advance, nor put clear mission tasks for them.
>
> The 'conspirators' did not do combat training of their 'fighters' (except for the Barkashov group of nationalists who had their own

program); as a result, raged pensioners-Stalinists and 15-year-old romantically-minded fools, not knowing that they should hide from bullets, stormed the Ostankino TV Centre.

The 'conspirators' did not prepare the 'allied' organizations for interaction, which resulted in permanent conflicts, for example, between the Anpilov group and the punks, between the Barkashov group and the leftists (anarchists and followers of Trotsky), etc. According to estimates of journalist Yuri Nersesov, twelve (!) competing and constantly interfering with each other 'defense headquarters' operated in the parliament building at the same time: Rutskoi's, Khasbulatov's, Voronin's, Barannikov's, Achalov's, Dunaev's, Makashov's, the 'Reform of the Army's deputy group's, the Union of Officers', etc.

The 'conspirators' neither conducted a focused campaign in the army ... nor ensured in advance support of specific commanders, promising high posts after winning the 'conspiracy'.

The 'conspirators' had prepared neither armored vehicles, nor sufficient number of firearms. The weapons they took possession of either were kept in the parliament building since August 1991, or belonged to the parliament security, or were seized from the enemy. To successfully counteract the enemy, they needed to have at least man-portable anti-tank weapons or at minimum sufficient amount of explosives. At the end of the twentieth century nobody engages in a 'pre-planned armed rebellion' without the tanks. Given that one of the leaders of the 'conspirators' was Alexandr Rutskoi, a military pilot, it would be logical to expect a particularly broad involvement of the Air Force in the 'conspiracy'. But nothing of that took place.

Clearly, the 'conspirators' themselves had no idea about the tactics of street fighting and did not teach their supporters to it: the 'barricades' they had erected were not an obstacle to the government vehicles; the concrete blocks, thrown around the parliament as 'defense' from the tanks, were placed quite mediocre and could not protect the building from the tank attack. Not to mention that the tanks did not need to approach the parliament for the shelling.

The 'conspirators' had captured and then resignedly released the riot police and military personnel of Dzerzhinsky Division, which was deployed near the parliament building. Had they really been the conspirators and planned all in advance, they would have disarmed the police and military, taken off all their body armor, shields, radio, and vehicles. Not to mention that the captured soldiers and the riot policemen could have been used as hostages or simply put in the windows of the building, making any assault impossible.

When the blockade of the parliament had been removed by the pro-parliament defenders, it was prudent in response to cordon off the City Hall, using the same barbed wire and watering machines, and cut off the Mayor's Office of energy and telephone networks; but nothing of that was done. Or they could have blocked with their armed units all exits from the Kremlin and continue negotiations with Yeltsin - but from a more powerful position. ...

Storming of the Ostankino TV Centre and the City Hall did not make any sense. Those were not strategically important objects but just symbols. ... Of course, television, as a 'means of mass destruction', plays a huge role in any conspiracy. Since majority of the population is suggestible and a significant part of it - very suggestible (in the era of the upheaval the number of highly suggestible people soars to 70-90%, according to some estimates), it is obvious that if the audience is methodically instilled any delusions for a long time (e.g. Khasbulatov is an alien, and Rutskoi is the Antichrist), then the people will eventually believe it. But capture of mass media should precede any coup. ...

Focused on Ostankino, the 'conspirators' ignored another TV centre ('Shabolovka'), which was probably even easier to capture, and they did not take control of radio stations and other news agencies.

Sending people far away - to Ostankino - the 'conspirators' did not pay attention to really important objects: the Board of Ministers and the Kremlin. Even if they had no power to capture the Kremlin, they could have cordoned off the government and disorganized its operations; ... the disruption could have been significant - the government would have been forced to focus on self-defense. ...

They forgot about vital, strategic assets like power stations, telephone exchange centers, water pumping and distribution stations, train stations, barracks of the Army and the Interior Ministry, the KGB complex, the Interior Ministry' building, police departments, military schools, airports, transport exchanges. The 'conspirators' did not even bother to seize the power station which supplied electricity to the parliament! [Though on September 26-27, 1994, General Makashov attempted to seize the headquarters and communication center of the Civil Defense; he successfully captured its underground office without any firing, but the center was already empty and abandoned.]

There was no attempt to seize weapons arsenals. ... The 'conspirators' had not sent any commissioners to the military units with relevant orders issued by General Achalov (or, even better, by Rutskoi as the Acting Chief Commander); though this measure could have been successful in at least one-third of the military divisions. It is well known that in some places the parliament defenders managed to convince some soldiers to give away their arms.

No attempt was made to capture ... the enemy leaders in order to disrupt their operations (Yeltsin as the 'former' President, Victor Chernomyrdin as the Prime Minister, Egor Gaidar as the former Prime Minister, Pavel Grachev as the Defense Minister) ... The fact that Yeltsin was not in Moscow on October 3 implies that he knew about the upcoming events and feared the 'non-standard' actions of the 'rebels'. ...

It is incomprehensible why the 'conspirators' did not leave the parliament building - a trap - to spread out in the uncontrolled city or to fly away, while it was possible, into one of the supporting regions. They could have seized an airplane - they had some armed units for that; and Rutskoi as a military pilot could have personally taken the helm of one of the aircrafts - his image would have only benefitted from that. ... The Supreme Soviet could easily gather in Novosibirsk, where it was supported by all branches of power, and formed a government plenipotentiary on the controlled area - there have been good examples of this kind: The Komuch [The Committee of Members of the All-Russian Constituent Assembly] in Samara in 1918, the Ufa Directorate in 1918, the Alexandr Kolchak's government in Omsk in 1918-1920. ...

Had there been a 'conspiracy', a 'pre-planned armed rebellion', these mistakes would have not been made...[23]

The entire defense of the parliament was based on the sanctity of then current constitution. The Supreme Soviet believed that the West and the United States in particular would recoil in horror from Yeltsin after learning that he violated the Constitution he had sworn allegiance to. The parliament also believed that the army would adhere to their oath to guard the constitutional order.[42]

Some political analysts argued that though 53 regions of Russia sided with the Supreme Soviet of the People's Deputies, this support was more declarative than practical: the regional elites just feared to lose their power if the Supreme Soviet was dissolved. None of the regions took drastic actions to support the parliament. There were neither strikes, nor blocking of highways and railways, nothing like that. The society met with indifference the eradication of the legislative branch. A short-term development of Russia in the direction of the parliamentary-presidential republic had ended. Apparently, the Soviet system instilled in Russian people a passive civil position to the authorities.[43]

Having eliminated the potential danger of overthrowing and the threat of criminal prosecution in connection with the "shock therapy", Yeltsin and his associates concentrated in their hands all branches of power - executive, legislative, and judicial - until the voting on the new constitution and elections of a new body of the Russian legislature in December of 1993. The executive branch of power seized an opportunity to rewrite the constitution the way they wanted.

The presidential draft of the new constitution was released for general discussion a month before the referendum, on November 10, 1993. However, as experts stated, the discussion did not happen because of the artificially upheld very tense political climate of fear, uncertainty and hopelessness, spawning apathy to the proposed constitution in a large part of the population.[44] According to the opinion polls, more than 50% of the population before the referendum did not read the text of the new draft. On December 12, 1993, 58% of electorate at the national referendum voted "for" the Yeltsin's constitution and 42% "against" it. There were serious allegations that the lists of voters were manipulated in the province to make the results legitimate.[44]

The Constitution of the Russian Federation that is currently in force was amended at the time of absolute presidential power and ensured for the future the president standing above all other power institutions. In accordance with the new constitution, the parliament (now called the State Duma) could not oppose the president any more.[44]

Who do we have to blame for the October 1993 tragedy? Primarily, ourselves for indifference, Boris Yeltsin and his government for unjustified killing, and, to a lesser degree, the parliament. The Supreme Soviet of the People's Deputies is responsible for not stopping Yeltsin's attempts to establish regime of personal power in 1992 and first half of 1993 when they voted on the president's impeachment. Alexandr Rutskoi and Ruslan Khasbulatov swore that they would fight for the freedom of Russia to death, but in the end they peacefully surrendered.

Events of October 3-4, 1993 left us with a bitter aftertaste. April 1993's referendum clearly demonstrated what the people of Russia wanted: the president and the parliament to work in tandem. Instead, Yeltsin seized all the power. Would it have been better for the country, if the Parliament had won? Igor Bunich, a known pro-Yeltsin publicist, in his book *Sword of the President*, written in the wake of the October 1993 events, said that if not for Yeltsin, Russia would not have existed anymore, agonizing in countless conflicts unleashed by vain and shallow unintelligent party warlords and khans. Yeltsin had more rights to rule Russia than any other former party official, and they recognized Yeltsin as the head of the state.[42] Bunich justified Yeltsin's "firm hand" ruling and admired his dictatorship inclinations. There might be some truth in his statement, but only little bit. At the time, we needed both: Yeltsin as the president and a strong, independent parliament.

Yeltsin's popularity rating dropped to 3% by 1996, the presidential election year. In the first round of the elections, Yeltsin got ahead of Gennady Zyuganov, the Communist Party leader, by meager 3%. In the second round, Yeltsin won about 54% of the total votes with solid support from all major Russian oligarchs. However, a number of journalists, political analysts, and historians (including known historian V. Nikonov, who was then the deputy chairman of the "All-Russian Movement for Support of Boris Yeltsin" and the head of the press center of Yeltsin's electoral headquarters) believe that the 1996 presidential campaign cannot be called democratic elections, because the president abused his absolute power. Yeltsin's electoral staff admitted widespread use of administrative resources, the fact that they exceeded many times the spending limits established by law for presidential candidates, and that virtually all of the mass media openly supported Yeltsin, except for a few communist newspapers published in small numbers.[]

What could have happened, had Yeltsin agreed to the pre-term presidential elections demanded by the parliament? Khasbulatov answered that question nineteen years later in his 2012' interview with journalist Sergei Korzun from the radio Echo Moskvy. Khasbulatov said that the Supreme Soviet, which possessed quite broad powers at the time, aimed at building normal capitalism. "I did not want the capitalism which has been built in Russia for as many as 20 years. Even being 'in hot delirium' I could not imagine that we would become the captives of such capitalism. ... Yeltsin ... understood nothing, he just commanded from above. ... He knew nothing what he talked about - except for human resource management. In that area he certainly kept all in hands, following the party's old habit. But economy or other matters - he did not want to deal with it. By the way, we would have worked well together with Yeltsin, if not for these permanent squeakers, snitches, and schemers..."[46]

In subsequent years, under the president Yeltsin's ruling, we went through devastating war in Chechnya, second wave of burglarious privatization, financial crisis, and default on state debts in 1998. The tragic decade for Russia had finally ended with Yeltsin's resignation on December 31, 1999.

Many of the opposition to the current President Vladimir Putin sided with Yeltsin in the 1993 clash. They reap what they have sown: they had shot the parliamentary republic in 1993, paving the way to the presidential dictatorship in Russia.

REPORTERS ABANDONED EVEN THE PRETENSE OF OBJECTIVITY

Jeff Cohen and Norman Solomon from the Fairness *&* Accuracy in Reporting brilliantly expressed[45] the gist of October 1993 revolt in Russia and response of western news agencies to it:

> When the Russian crisis began, CBS anchor Dan Rather suggested (9/21/93) that Boris Yeltsin 'didn't go far enough' in getting rid of the 'hard-liners'. But how does a president legally get rid of elected members of parliament?
>
> President Yeltsin did it by simply dissolving parliament on Sept. 21, a blatantly unconstitutional move that won immediate support from the Clinton administration -- and immediate excuses from most U.S. media. A New York Times editorial (9/22/93) referred to Yeltsin's dissolution of parliament as 'a Democrat's Coup'.
>
> With the Clinton White House backing Yeltsin's every move, including ultimately the assault on Russia's 'White House', U.S. reporters abandoned even the pretense of objectivity. 'Hard-liners' became the universal description for the leaders of parliament, who were rarely quoted explaining their reasons for opposing Yeltsin. As the Russian parliament burned, the Christian Science Monitor declared, in a front-page news article (10/5/93), that 'it was clear that the government of President Boris Yeltsin had little choice but to respond with overwhelming force'.

Were Yeltsin's opponents really merely 'an unruly band of malcontents --ranging from anti-Semitic fascists and nationalists to fervent monarchists and hard-line Stalinists', as USA Today (10/4/93) reported? In fact, the leaders of the opposition were Yeltsin's men. Yeltsin hand-picked Ruslan Khasbulatov to be his successor as parliament speaker when he ran for president, and chose Aleksandr Rutskoi as his vice presidential running-mate. Both Khasbulatov and Rutskoi were Communists for most of their lives - but so was Yeltsin, who served for years as the Communist mayor of Moscow.

Elected in fairly free elections in 1990 near the end of the Gorbachev era, the 'hard-line' leaders of parliament defied Gorbachev and the Communist Party by selecting Yeltsin as the chair of parliament. During the 1991 coup by Communist apparatchiks against Gorbachev, the parliament provided sanctuary to Yeltsin, helping to stave off the coup. A few months later, the parliament ratified Yeltsin's decision to abolish the Soviet Union, and then gave Yeltsin decree-making power for a year to implement his severe economic program. In a real sense, this had been Yeltsin's parliament.

What drove Yeltsin and the parliament apart was the economic 'shock treatment' prescribed by the World Bank and the International Monetary Fund. Under Yeltsin, state possessions -- including oil and other natural resources -- are being rapidly privatized, mainly by being sold off to Western companies. Hailed as 'free-market economic reforms' by U.S. and Western European media, this process has also spurred corruption, unemployment and economic chaos.

The economic dislocation caused by these kinds of 'reforms' has caused many of Yeltsin's former allies to turn against him. Although 'democrat' and 'free marketer' are often equated, events since the dissolution of parliament - particularly the postponement of presidential elections until 1996 - have borne out the fact that Yeltsin is more committed to privatization than democratization. And most U.S. mass media seem to share that preference.[45]

NO MAN IS A PROPHET IN HIS OWN COUNTRY

The consequences of the path the country was choosing in the beginning of 1990s were foreseen by some economists in Russia, such as Mark Golansky. In 1987 the Deputy Chairman of the State Committee for Labor and Social Problems (Goskomtrud) invited economist Mark Golansky to speak at the meeting of the Council. Golansky's report was based on the fact that capitalism is much more efficient than socialism in the use of resources, production of various goods and services. But socialism better supports social justice, more effectively solves mobilization tasks when achievement of a goal in a specified period is more important than resource expenditure.

All of the conclusions Golansky meticulously justified with the results of his economic-mathematical modeling. He predicted in 1987:

> Switching to capitalism will completely upset functioning of the Soviet economy. The country will be affected by large scale unemployment, it will suffer from the growth of social ills, falling birth rates, rising crime and mass emigration. The plight of the economy will be accompanied by national disintegration and virtual collapse of the state. Therefore, the expectations that introduction of private ownership and free market in the Soviet Union will be salutary remedy to the economic ills is deeply flawed. The shift towards capitalism won't bring any good to the Soviet Union. All of the current economic systems of the country will be destroyed and replaced by a symbiosis of resource monopolies, enclaves of transnational corporations, and small-scale domestic production.

> The transition to capitalism will knock the economy out of operation state for a long time, and its effects can be equated to a catastrophe, a disaster.[17]

As we see now, his model turned out to be visionary and accurately described what happened to the country in 1990s.

The report impressed the Deputy Chairman of Goskomtrud so much that he sent it to the Chairman of the USSR Council of Ministers Nikolai Ryzhkov, but received no response. Then he sent the report to one of Gorbachev advisers - economist Stanislav Shatalin. Shatalin took the material seriously and offered to publish in the main party journal The Communist. The economic department of The Communist was headed by Yegor Gaidar, the future prime minister in Yeltsin's government and the chief ideologist of the "shock therapy". Yegor Gaidar and Mark Golansky met and conversed for many hours; Gaidar popularly "explained" to the professor of economics Golansky that he knew nothing about either the macroeconomics, or the free market economy, or modeling. Gaidar refused to publish an article in the journal and put his hand to ensure that Golansky acquired reputation of an eccentric dilettante whose works did not deserve attention.

The Golansky book was published in 1992, to a great extent due to help of Chairman of the Supreme Soviet Ruslan Khasbulatov. Khasbulatov was a well-known economist, doctor and professor of economics, the head of the Department of the World Economy in the famous Plekhanov Institute in Moscow.

In mid-80s Golansky made even more surprising forecasts regarding fate of capitalism in the XXI century. He pointed that there were objective barriers to the development of capitalism. According to his results, global capitalism will continue to develop from 1985 to 2010, although the pace of economic growth will be permanently slowing. And from 2010 the world capitalist system will be falling into the deep systemic crisis, which won't have solution within the framework of the market economy. Golansky forewarned that the way out of the crisis would be found in the worldwide implementation of central planning and economic modeling, as well as in the displacement of the free market practices in key industries and sectors by planning and imperious regulations; the planning in the future would be implemented through both direct assignments and financial and credit levers. As is usually the case with the prophets, Mark Golansky died without receiving any recognition.[47]

EPILOGUE

Yeltsin's victory has driven our country onto the path of wild, corrupt and ruthless capitalism. I believe that one day Russia will return to the socialist economy refined from the rigid political ideology, because it is the most humane form of economy of all known to the mankind. Alexandr Zinoviev, a famous Soviet dissident in the past, confessed in his book *The Russian Tragedy (The Death of Utopia)*:[8]

> The ideals of communism are not feasible, but these ideals raised our lives to the greatest heights of historical romanticism ... Russian Communism was a random gift of history to the Russians. They did not manage to save it. If the Russians survive and if they happen to live again under the communism, it will come to them from the outside. ...

Now the overwhelming majority of people associate with the word 'communism' only negative phenomena of the Soviet period. A grand falsification of the Soviet history is going on along with the anti-communist propaganda. New generations will not know the truth about the communism. Efforts of millions of people will disappear without a trace. To uphold positive achievements of the Soviet period as achievements of the communism is impossible. Having opened the communist way of evolution for the humanity, Russia failed to defend it, but betrayed and discredited it for a long time, if not forever.[8]

RUSSIA IN NUMBERS

The territory of Russia is over 17 million square kilometers, but 85% of its area is unsuitable for year round comfortable living. 8,099 glaciers and permafrost in Siberia and the Far East take 65% of its territory, marshes and wetlands occupy almost 22%, rivers and lakes - about 4%.

The growing season in most parts of Russia is 2-4 months (in Europe or in the United States - 8-9 months). Up to 70% of Russia's food needs are covered by imports. Compared to the Soviet times the number of herds decreased (in millions of heads): sheep and goat - from 67 to 9.7; pig - from 33.2 to 8.5; cow - from 20.6 to 12.

Russia produces up to 2% of the global GDP. The main export items are gas and oil - 70%, primary metals - 15%, logs - 10%, equipment, weapons and technology - less than 5%. Russia accounts for 5% of the world oil and 30% of the world gas reserves. The Russian oil production cost $ 14 a barrel, more than three times higher than Kuwait's.

1.5% of the Russian population own 50% of the national wealth. Russian billionaires are paying the lowest taxes in the world (13%). 90.9% of the population teeter around the poverty line with varying degrees of success.

> The majority of the Russian population is concentrated in the triangle whose vertices are St.-Petersburg in the north, Novorossiysk in the south and Irkutsk in the east. Siberia, covering an area of nearly 3/4 of Russia, is home to less than a quarter of its population, mostly along the Trans-Siberian Railway. In the last twenty years, 11,000 villages and 290 towns were abandoned in Siberia.[48]

WORKS CITED

1. Пенсионный фонд Российской Федерации *Среднемесячная заработная плата в стране.* URL: http://www.pfr.kirov.ru/node/51 (*Average salary in the country* by The Pension Fund of the Russian Federation). Retrieved 1 March 2013.

2. Тарасов А.М. *Миллионер.* - Издательство Вагриус, 2004 - 672 с. (*Millioner* by A.M. Tarasov, Vagrius, 2004 - 672 p.).

3. *Collapse of an Empire: Lessons for Modern Russia*, by Yegor Gaidar, Brookings Institution Press, 2007.

4. Черных Е. *Егор Лигачёв: В Кремле не нашлось бойцов, чтобы убрать Горбачева и спасти страну!* - Комсомольская Правда, 29 декабря 2011. URL: http://www.kp.by/daily/25813.3/2791269/ (*Yegor Ligachev: The Kremlin Had Not Found Fighters to Remove Gorbachev and Save the Country!* By E. Chernyh, Komsomolskaya Pravda, 29 December, 2011). Retrieved 29 December 2011.

5. *Godfather of the Kremlin: Boris Berezovsky and the Looting of Russia* by Paul Klebnikov, 2000.

6. Госкомстат *Российский статистический ежегодник* — 1997, стр. 554. (*Russian Statistical Yearbook* by Goskomstat, 1997, p.554).

7. *Ельцин, Борис Николаевич.* Материал из Википедии — свободной энциклопедии. URL:

http://ru.wikipedia.org/wiki/%D0%95%D0%BB%D1%8C%D1%86
%D0%B8%D0%BD,_%D0%91%D0%BE%D1%80%D0%B8%D1%
81_%D0%9D%D0%B8%D0%BA%D0%BE%D0%BB%D0%B0%D
0%B5%D0%B2%D0%B8%D1%87 (*Yeltsin, Boris Nikolaevich* by Wikipedia). Retrieved 1 February, 2013.

8. Зиновьев А.А. *Русская трагедия: гибель утопии*, 2002 - 480 с. (*The Russian Tragedy: The Death of Utopia* by A.A. Zinoviev, 2002 - 480 p.).

9. Михайлов А. *Мифология приватизации*. URL: http://www.gazeta.ru/column/mikhailov/3405772.shtml (*Mythology of Privatization* by A. Mikhailov). Retrieved 1 March 2013.

10. Пешков А. *"Газпром" - это хорошо или не очень?* URL: http://www.trading-world.ru/index.php?name=news&op=printe&id=172 *("Gazprom" - Is it Good or Not?* by A. Peshkov, 14.08.2008). Retrieved 1 March 2013.

11. Хинштейн А. *Ельцин. Кремль. История болезни.* - Изд-во Олма Медиа Групп, 2007 - 576 с. (*Yeltsin. Kremlin. Medical History* by A. Khinshtein, 2007 - 576 p.).

12. Константинов А. *Бандитский Петербург.* - Изд-во Амфора, 2009 - 480 с. (*Criminal Petersburg* by A. Konstantinov. - Amfora, 2009 - 480 p.).

13. Федеральная служба государственной статистики (Росстат). *Россия в цифрах 2008 - Статистика Росстата*. Росстат, 2008 - 507 с. (*Russia by the Numbers 2008 - Rosstat* by Federal Statistics Service (RosStat), 2008 - 507 p.).

14. Карышев В. *Русская мафия 1988-2007.* - Изд-во Эксмо, 2008 - 832с. (*The Russian Mafia 1988-2007* by V. Karyshev. - Eksmo, 2008 - 832 p.).

15. Иванов А. *Заказные преступления: убийства, кражи, грабежи.* - Минск, 1998 - 158 с. (*Ordered Crimes: Murders, Thefts, Robberies,* by A.

Ivanov. -Minsk: 1998 - 158 p.).

16. Веллер М. *Великий последний шанс*. - Изд-во АСТ, Харвест, 2005 - 464 с. (*The Great Last Chance* by M. Veller. - AST, Harvest, 2005 - 464 p.).

17. Калабеков И.Г. *Российские реформы в цифрах и фактах* (справочное издание). - М.: РУСАКИ, 2007 - 288 с. (*Russian Reforms in Facts and Figures* by I.G. Kalabekov. M., Rusaki, 2007 - 288 p.).

18. Реформы правительства Ельцина — Гайдара. Материал из Википедии — свободной энциклопедии. URL: http://ru.wikipedia.org/wiki/%D0%A0%D0%B5%D1%84%D0%BE%D1%80%D0%BC%D1%8B_%D0%BF%D1%80%D0%B0%D0%B2%D0%B8%D1%82%D0%B5%D0%BB%D1%8C%D1%81%D1%82%D0%B2%D0%B0_%D0%95%D0%BB%D1%8C%D1%86%D0%B8%D0%BD%D0%B0_%E2%80%94_%D0%93%D0%B0%D0%B9%D0%B4%D0%B0%D1%80%D0%B0 (*Reforms by Yeltsin-Gaidar Government* by Wikipedia). Retrieved March 1, 2013.

19. С. П. Пыхтин, "Советская Россия", 17.10.92. Цитируется по Савельев А. *Мятеж номенклатуры. Москва 1990-1993*, 1995. URL: http://savelev.ru/book/?ch=221&mode=reply (Sergey Pykhtin, Soviet Russia, 17.10.92. Cited from *Mutiny of the Nomenclature. Moscow 1990-1993* by A. Saveliev, 1995).

20. Хасбулатов Р. И. *Великая Российская трагедия*. - Изд-во ТОО "Симс", 1994 - 876 с. (*The Great Russian Tragedy* by R.I. Khasbulatov. - ТОО "Sims", 1994 - 876 p.).

21. *Разгон Верховного Совета России*. Материал из Википедии — свободной энциклопедии. URL: http://ru.mobile.wikipedia.org/wiki/%D0%A0%D0%B0%D1%81%D1%81%D1%82%D1%80%D0%B5%D0%BB_%D0%BF%D0%B0%D1%80%D0%BB%D0%B0%D0%BC%D0%B5%D0%BD%D1%82%D0%B0_%D0%B8%D0%B7_%D1%82%D0%B0%D0%BD%D0

%BA%D0%BE%D0%B2 (*Dissolution of the Supreme Soviet of Russia* by Wikipedia). Retrieved May 1, 2013.

22. Касьянов В. *Расстрелянная Россия*. - Журнал Самиздат, 17/02/2013.   URL: http://samlib.ru/w/wladimir_kasxjanow/rasstrel_rossii.shtml (*Shot Down Russia* by V. Kasyanov. - Samizdat, 2013).

23. Тарасов А.Н. *Провокация. Версия событий 3–4 октября 1993 г. в Москве.-*
М.: Центр новой социологии и изучения практической политики "Феникс", 1993 (*The Provocation. A Version of Events in Moscow on October 3–4, 1993* by A.N. Tarasov. — Moscow: Center for New Sociology and Research in Applied Politics "Phoenix", 1993).

24. *Доклад Комиссии Государственной Думы Федерального Собрания Российской Федерации по дополнительному изучению и анализу событий, происходивших в городе Москве 21 сентября 5 октября 1993 года*. URL: http://duma2.garant.ru/struct/temp_com.htm, http://rudocs.exdat.com/docs/index-47026.html (*Report of the Commission of the State Duma of the Federal Assembly of the Russian Federation for further study and analysis of the events that took place in Moscow on September 21 October 5, 1993*). Retrieved 1 May 2013.

25. Агентство федеральных расследований *Октябрьское восстание 1993 года*, 21.11.2007. URL: http://1993.sovnarkom.ru/TEXT/STATYI/flb_ru_2006.htm (*October Uprising in 1993* by The Agency of Federal Investigation, 21 November 2007). Retrieved 4 October 2011.

26. *Защитниками "Белого дома" и теми, кто стрелял по нему, управляли из одного центра*, 4 октября 2011. URL: http://informacia.ru/topsecret/1/1863-966.html (*Defenders of the White House and Those Who Fired on Them Were Controlled from the Same Centre*, 4 October, 2011). Retrieved 1 June 2013.

27. *Первый выстрел и первая кровь. Москва, Останкино, 3 октября 1993 года, 19:30.* URL: http://www.memo.ru/hr/hotpoints/moscow93/cher93/left3.htm (*The First Shot and The First Blood. Moscow, Ostankino, October 3, 1993. 19:30*).

28. Иванов И. *Хроника государственного переворота.* - Изд-во Палея, 1995 - 502 с. (*Anafema: Chronicles of the Coup D'état*, by Ivan Ivanov, 1995 - 502 p.).

29. Прошкин Л. *Штурм которого не было. Неизвестные страницы уголовного дела N 18/123669-93.* - "Совершенно секретно", 1998 - N 9. (*The Assault That Did Not Take Place. Unknown Pages of the Criminal Case N 18/123669-93* by L. Proshkin. - The Top Secret, 1998 - N 9).

30. Ельцин Б.Н. *Записки президента.* - М., Изд-во Огонек, 1994 - 512 с. (*Notes of the President* by B.N. Yeltsin, 1994 - 512 p.).

31. *Stray Shot Killed American Lawyer During Fight At Television*, by Los Angeles Times, October 6, 1993.

32. *Rory Peck* by Wikipedia. URL: http://en.wikipedia.org/wiki/Rory_Peck. Retrieved on February 1, 2013.

33. *1993 Russian Constitutional Crisis* by Wikipedia. URL: http://en.wikipedia.org/wiki/1993_Russian_constitutional_crisis - Retrieved March 1, 2013.

34. Фочкин О., Болгаров Д. *Белые пятна черного октября 93-го.* - "Московский Комсомолец", 03.10.2003 (*White Spots of the Black October of 1993* by O. Fochkin, D. Bolgarov, Moskovsky Komsomolets, 03.10.2003).

35. Шевченко В.А. *Забытые жертвы октября 1993 года.* - Тула: Гриф и К, 2010 - 128 с. (*Forgotten Victims of October 1993* by V. Shevchenko,

2010 - 128 p.).

36. Коржаков А. *Борис Ельцин: от рассвета до заката.* - Изд-во Интербук, 1997 - 480 с. (*Boris Yeltsin: From Dawn Till Sunset* by A. Korzhakov. - Interbuk, 1997 - 480 p.).

37. Савельев А. Н. *Как убивали СССР. Кто стал миллиардером.* - Изд-во "Книжный Мир", 2012. (*How the Soviet Union Was Killed. Who Became Billionaires* by A.N. Saveliev, 2012).

38. Игонин Ю. *Как это было.* - Речь, № 1, ноябрь 1993 (*How It Was* by Yu. Igonin, The Speech, N1, November 1993).

39. Кононенко В. *За что нас расстреляли.* - «Советская Россия» № 122 (10985), 23 декабря 1993. (*For What We Were Shot Down* by V. Kononenko, Soviet Russia, N122, December 23, 1993).

40. Попов А.Б. *Затмение.* - Коммунист Дубны, 2011.- Сентябрь №9 (92). URL: http://www.kprf-dubna.su/new_page_kDsent2011.htm (*Brain Clouding* by A.B. Popov, Dubna Communist, 2011. - September N 9 (92)). Retrieved March 1, 2013.

41. Прошкин Л. *Черный октябрь. Часть 1.* - Экспресс-газета, 3 октября 2008 - N 39 (712). URL: http://www.eg.ru/daily/politics/11203/ (*Black October. Part 1* by L. Proshkin. - Express-Newspaper, 3 October 2008 - N 39 (712)). Retrieved 1 June 2013.

42. Бунич И. *Меч президента.* - Изд-во Эксмо, 2004 - 154 с. (*Sword of the President* by Igor Bunich, Eksmo, 2004 - 154 p.).

43. Дюков К.В. *Проблемы становления Российской государственности в 90-х гг. XX в.* URL: http://www.superinf.ru/view_helpstud.php?id=3948 (*Problems of the Formation of Russian Statehood in 1990s* by K.V. Dyukov). Retrieved on Feb 1, 2013.

44. Государственный строй. Конституция РФ 1993. URL: http://www.novrosen.ru/Russia/state/constitution.htm (*1993 Constitution of the Russian Federation*). Retrieved Feb 1, 2013.

45. *Are All Yeltsin Critics 'Hard-Line' -- Or Is That Just the U.S. Media's Party Line?* By Jeff Cohen and Norman Solomon, Fairness & Accuracy In Reporting, Jan 01 1994. URL: http://fair.org/extra-online-articles/are-all-yeltsin-critics-quothard-linequot-or-is-that-just-the-u-s-medias-party-line/. Retrieved on Jun 1, 2013.

46. Корзун С. *Без Дураков. Интервью с Р. Хазбулатовым.* - Радио "Эхо Москвы", 19:05 18 ноября 2012. URL: http://echo.msk.ru/programs/korzun/950965-echo/ (*No Fools. Interview with Ruslan Khasbulatov* by S. Korzun, Radio Station Echo of Moscow, 19:05 November 18, 2012).

47. Черных Е. *Советский ученый предсказал мировой кризис и сырьевое проклятие России четверть века назад.* - Комсомольская правда, 28 мая 2013. URL: http://www.kp.ru/daily/26082/2985758/ (*A Soviet Scientist Foresaw The World Crisis and Resource Curse for Russia Quarter of Century Ago* by Eugene Chernyh, Komsomolskaya Pravda, 28 May 2013.) Retrieved on May 28, 2013.

48. Агентство РиФ *Население России. Статистика, факты, комментарии, прогнозы,* 2011. URL: http://www.rf-agency.ru/acn/stat_ru (*The Population of Russia. Stats, Facts, Analyses, Forecasts* by Agency RiF, 2011). Retrieved on May 1, 2012.

CPSIA information can be obtained at www.ICGtesting.com
Printed in the USA
LVOW13s1207120214

373410LV00022B/1058/P